# THE PERILS OF GIRLHOOD

AMERICAN LIVES

Series editor: Tobias Wolff

"Through a crystalline rendering of an eighties girlhood (bran cereal and the Barbie Style Head, Judy Blume and Jean M. Auel, aerosol hairspray and Zinka, Judd Nelson and Rob Lowe, too much exercise and too little food) and onward into a writing career and motherhood, the essays in Melissa Fraterrigo's *The Perils of Girlhood* navigate the complexity of a life lived in a female body with the kind of clarity and empathy that both brings me back—I mean, Fraterrigo gets me—and helps me to see a way forward."

—JILL CHRISTMAN, author of *If This Were Fiction: A Love Story in Essays*

"This collection is a subtle subversion of the conservative political narrative that women's lives are inconsequential, and somehow interchangeable. These compelling essays about sexuality, home life, coming of age, and the interior life are not always in-your-face, but they are always in-your-soul."

—SUE WILLIAM SILVERMAN, author of *Acetylene Torch Songs: Writing True Stories to Ignite the Soul*

"*The Perils of Girlhood* is a reckoning with self and world, with girlhood as well as womanhood—and motherhood—and the violence that hovers at all times around the periphery and occasionally breaks through. Marked by their raw honesty and precision, these essays transcend the purely personal and speak to the complexities and challenges of being a woman in our current cultural moment."

—STEVE EDWARDS, author of *Breaking into the Backcountry*

"Melissa Fraterrigo writes of a friend, 'Near her, everything loosens and I feel sixteen again,' which is how I feel reading (and rereading) *The Perils of Girlhood*. How I wish this book had been given to me when I was a girl—to make sense of the simmering frustrations with wanting and resenting male attention, with accepting others' anger while denying one's own, with trying to be agreeable and likable and perfect. *The Perils of Girlhood* is a necessary book that I will recommend for years to come."

—JEANNIE VANASCO, author of *Things We Didn't Talk About When I Was a Girl*

"This gorgeous, shattering, hopeful, sorrowful, soulful book is about the perils (and glories) of girlhood, yes, but also of motherhood and daughterhood, womanhood, life. I dare anyone to read it without a frequent—maybe constant—shiver of *oh yes, me too*. Whether Melissa Fraterrigo is writing about the excruciations of adolescence, the highs and lows of love and marriage, self-image, friendship, extreme dieting, or the daily just-below-the-surface drumbeat of worry that's so often baked into motherhood (not an inclusive list!), she is writing from the heart, beautifully and heartbreakingly and oh-so-smartly."

—MICHELLE HERMAN, author of *If You Say So*

"In this striking collection, Melissa Fraterrigo offers intimate essays examining her youthful fears and desires and the complex challenges facing her now as she parents twin girls. *The Perils of Girlhood* is an essential meditation on how we raise our daughters, in a voice that is clear, honest, and wise."

—DINTY W. MOORE, author of *Between Panic and Desire*

# THE PERILS
# OF GIRLHOOD

*A Memoir in Essays*

**MELISSA FRATERRIGO**

UNIVERSITY OF NEBRASKA PRESS

*Lincoln*

The University of Nebraska Press is part of a land-grant institution with campuses and programs on the past, present, and future homelands of the Pawnee, Ponca, Otoe-Missouria, Omaha, Dakota, Lakota, Kaw, Cheyenne, and Arapaho Peoples, as well as those of the relocated Ho-Chunk, Sac and Fox, and Iowa Peoples.

∞

For customers in the EU with safety/GPSR concerns, contact:
gpsr@mare-nostrum.co.uk
Mare Nostrum Group BV
Mauritskade 21D
1091 GC Amsterdam
The Netherlands

Library of Congress Control Number: 2025010539

Designed and set in Adobe Jenson Pro by Katrina Noble.

*For my girlfriends*

I lock my door at night
I keep my mouth shut tight
I practice all my moves
I memorize their stupid rules
I make myself their friend
I'll show them just how far I can bend

— *"Help Me Mary," Liz Phair*

You mean to say that after all you are really going to be the kind of woman who the baker won't let near the bread?

— *"Girl," Jamaica Kincaid*

# CONTENTS

# THE PERILS OF GIRLHOOD

# PRELUDE

In my forties, buzzy from a second glass of wine with a high school friend I haven't seen for years, I confide that the summer before our freshman year my swim coach pulled me into the pool and pressed himself against me.

"Oh, my god! That must have been so exciting!" she says, leaning forward.

"No," I say. "It wasn't like that. It was terrifying. I didn't know what to do."

And, suddenly, on this restaurant patio, here she is: my adolescent self. His hands are pinned to me, breath taut in my chest. I want to scream but I can't. I don't want to make a scene.

I watch my friend's face, one that is as familiar to me as my own. I need her to understand, need to see my fear reflected back at me.

She grabs my hands. "I shouldn't have said that. I'm sorry. I'm so sorry that happened to you."

"It's okay," I say, taking back my hands. "It was a long time ago. It didn't matter." I sip my wine. Ask about her sons. She wants to know about my daughters. They are fourteen and in eighth grade with hair that swings down their backs, laughter like spun candy. Now my husband and I stand outside their closed bedroom doors, ask to be let in.

Once they were little girls.

After my friend and I go our separate ways, the conversation lingers, and as I drive home in the dark with the windows down, the air balmy, clouds ruffled like waves, I replay my words. *It didn't matter,* which is almost *I* didn't matter, a whole other peril.

Out the window the clouds split, baring a slice of moon as bright as the sun. A song from the '80s comes on the radio and I tap to the beat, a long-ago rhythm of memory alive in my body.

# COACH MATT

On the first day of the summer 1987 swim season, a college-aged guy in flip-flops with electric blue eyes stood beside Mrs. Renolds, the team president. Our regular coach, who taught at the high school, was nowhere to be seen. Mrs. Renolds introduced Matt, a student from the University of Kentucky, as our coach. This new coach had blond hair and wore a U2 T-shirt.

It felt odd from the start.

"This is Coach Bedar," she said. "He's home for the summer from college and we're so happy to have him here." Mrs. Renolds looked his way and giggled, her stomach jostling in ropy swells she failed to notice.

"Coach Matt is fine," he said and gave us a little wave.

Mrs. Renolds told us to have a good practice and left the pool deck, steel door clanging shut. During the school year there were anywhere from thirty to forty kids on the team. Attendance dwindled in the summer. Now I was one of ten kids standing around the TF South High School pool and the oldest there. I'd just finished the eighth grade and would be starting high school in the fall.

I stood there and shivered in my suit. I was nearly naked, but my bareness didn't register until now.

Coach Matt clapped his hands. "Okay. Let's get to work. We'll start with land training." He told us to do thirty sit-ups. I took my place on the deck, held my head and touched my elbows to bent knees. Coach Matt seemed cool, something I wasn't used to thinking about during swim practice. With each sit-up, the fabric of my suit puckered, then flattened. Aware that Coach Matt was watching us, I willed myself to move faster.

Push-ups followed. We stretched our arms by pressing our palms onto the tiled walls and turning our bodies in the opposite direction. When the balls of our shoulders looked like they were ready to snap, Coach Matt yelled, "Five-hundred warm-up! Everyone in!"

The water felt deliciously cool against my skin. That summer the entire Chicago area was accosted by a heat wave. Day after day the thermometer edged into the 90s, accompanied by a humidity that made it feel as if I were breathing through a straw.

As I pushed off the wall, everything faded away. I focused on the beat of my kick, watched the bubbles speed past my hands as I pushed them beneath the surface. During practice, when I had a definite goal, a certain number of 200s or 50s on a particular pace, my thoughts wandered. I'd push myself to keep with the white kick of the swimmer in front of me, while thinking about what I'd eaten for lunch, perhaps the book I was currently reading. I was obsessed with *The Clan of the Cave Bear* by Jean Auel, a spanning saga that took place during the dawn of mankind when a girl is orphaned after an earthquake and must fight for her survival. I loved stories like this—where the character relies upon the skills she didn't know she had to outwit the storm and slay the beast. I imagined everything would be easier if I also possessed some unique power.

I dreamed of becoming a writer. I kept a journal, just a plain-lined notebook, but in it I could write down all my frustrations and concerns. No matter what ideas occupied my mind when I started, I always ended in a different place. Writing felt good. And so did swimming. I'd sometimes imagine a driver pulling up as I rode my bike home from practice and rolling down his window. He'd tell me he'd seen me swim, and with the right training I could be an Olympian.

I'd then rush into our tiny bungalow shouting the news to my parents. They'd hug me, and my mom, who had recently taken a job as a school nurse, would look up from her papers and ask, "Who is he?" Then I'd show them his business card and even my dad—who often said the only people you could trust in life were your family— would put aside the newspaper, pleasure right there on his face.

Something else was happening, though. My body felt different than it used to, even while moving through the water. My breasts were coming in—little mounded nubs. I'd begun to shave using my mother's razor on my nonexistent leg hairs. I kept this a secret until my mom noticed the row of bandages on my shins and shared this with my oldest female cousin, who took me into our aunt's bathroom and showed me her legs during a family party.

She propped her foot on the sink next to the soap dish and pushed her pants over her knee. "See that?" She took my hand and ran it along the skin, the hair on them like tiny quills.

"I have to shave every day or this is how it feels."

I understood that this was supposed to discourage me from shaving. Only it had the opposite result: I'd gathered a lifetime of details about what it meant to be a woman and now, in the months before I would begin high school, I felt the pulsing need to apply everything I'd gleaned.

Coach Matt drove to Lansing each day from Chicago, the windows of his hatchback down, music up. Queen and the Rolling Stones, Rush and The Police. He wore Umbro shorts and a thin lace of leather knotted one wrist. He carried himself as if he didn't care what anyone else thought. A revolutionary idea. My sister and I had the same dark hair. People would often call me by her name. This happened so frequently I began to believe others *wanted* me to be her. My older brother, Michael, was a talented swimmer in his own right, eventually taking his high school team to State; Beth was two years younger than me and aced every report card and had recently begun dancing on pointe. My parents' faces lit up while witnessing her feats. I couldn't offer them such accomplishments, which aggravated my own ability to please myself. The closest I came to contentment arrived at the pool.

During practice, Coach Matt would stand poolside and mime a stroke, pushing up on the balls of his feet, the muscles in his calves popping like apples. He called me over to the side of the pool between sets and demonstrated how to extend my reach and improve my breaststroke—his event. Sometimes it seemed like he spent more time with me than the other swimmers.

After one grueling practice, he took me aside and asked, "Don't you want to go to State?"

I swallowed, unsure of myself. He stood close, nearly the same height as me. The blue of his eyes matched the water in the deep end. "I'm not even on the high school team," I said.

"You'll get on the team. But you've got to work harder. It's not going to just come to you."

His words settled in my mind and I realized he saw me as promising. Maybe I would make State and earn a scholarship. What if I ended up at his college?

The thought alone made me smile. But before that, I would need to compete in meets and swim against other girls. I loathed such stand-offs and the possibility I might fall short. I had much more work to do.

One day, Coach Matt barked a pre-swimming warm-up that would take place on land. "Everyone, find a partner for sit-ups." The other swimmers paired off and I stood there—alone.

"Let's go." Coach Matt directed me to sit, said he'd hold my feet.

I paused, looked at him, confused. I'd never seen him partner with any of my teammates.

"Sit." He said again.

I eased down, the tile warm and dry. I looked at my legs, unsure where to place my eyes. There I was on the deck in my practice suit, air from the vent beat down as he grasped my ankles and the rubber band from his watch flicked my foot. I felt different. Older? I had my period that day and worried the string of my tampon might be noticeable. "We'll do as many as we can in a minute," he announced to everyone. "Ready? Go!"

I tried to keep perfect form as I flattened my back and sat up, hands fastened to the rear of my head. I worked hard to seem strong and also not fart.

"Come on," he said, and counted: "Six, seven, eight." His head was right there, lingering in the space above my legs, a place I hadn't really considered.

I'd begun to wear sunglasses that summer. Cheap plastic frames I purchased at the flea market. They kept bugs from flying into my eyes as I rode my bike to or from practice. Once I arrived on 116th Street, I'd steer onto the gravel shoulder determined to keep the wheels of my ten-speed straight as the cars approached. But then the cars would honk their horns, a passenger waving his arms out the window as they passed. The first few times I thought there was something wrong but gradually I realized it was the driver or his passenger's way of getting my attention. No matter how often it happened I always jumped, frightened and enthralled.

With each bike ride I began to sense something new about myself, like a birthday gift that had been pushed to the back of my closet and only recently opened: men might find me attractive. Boys in my class, not so much, but strangers in cars on the highway saw something in me. I felt the burbling of this power inside me. It would take years for me to fully believe it, but for someone who had longed to be good at something, I glimpsed that perhaps I had finally found it.

While vacationing on the beach or dragging my feet alongside my mother's grocery cart at the store, I noticed glances from men. Those looks straightened my shoulders. Someone kept watch of me. I was worth watching.

Once I became aware of such glances, I turned this study onto myself.

When I wasn't at swim practice, I could be found in my room, often staring at myself in the floor-length mirror at the back of my door. Around this time, I'd begun dieting, watching my weight, just like my mother who went regularly to her meetings at TOPS—Take Off Pounds Sensibly. She tracked her daily calories on a Xeroxed sheet: Images of a fish, a loaf of bread, a carrot, and an apple alongside the corresponding boxes for protein, carbohydrates, vegetables, and fruits.

As hungry as I was, it was the mirror that kept me going. I'd stand before it most days and memorize the space between my thighs. After this I'd soothe myself with a routine of a hundred scissor-kicks. Lying on my back with legs extended inches from the ground, I'd lift my head then move my legs in and out while keeping my stomach muscles engaged, everything ramrod straight.

Alone in my bedroom, I was able to focus. I'd take my journal from under the mattress of my bed and I'd write about the kids at school, my parents' preference for my sister, and my growing crush on Coach Matt. Each swim practice became an opportunity to memorize him further. Sometimes I wrote directly to Coach Matt and asked, *"When you see me, what do you feel?"*

I'd had a crush on a classmate for much of junior high, but with Coach Matt the stakes seemed higher. I was entranced by him—the way that his hips lead as he moved, the cut of his biceps. Everything about his body announced that he was in charge.

As the summer went on, Coach Matt's hair became more golden, the humidity sweeping it into waves. His skin bronzed and his eyes turned a more intense blue. Each time I saw him was a chance to further take in all his details: The Pink Floyd T-shirts, the rock music he played before turning off his car. A fine smattering of hair rested on the tops of his wrists just like a man. When I wasn't at swim practice, I pulled out these details, turned them over in my mind. I understood my parents' pain, their desire to stand out, to have more money, a bigger house. All adults craved something and now I searched for this in Coach Matt as well.

Sometimes at the end of practice he would direct us to the deep end of the pool where he'd lead us in games. When we played shark, he joined in. During the game, swimmers stood along the perimeter of the deep end while one swimmer—the shark—treaded in the water and once everyone dove in, tried to tag as many "fish" as possible. Once you were tagged, you became a shark and the game went on until there were no fish left. Coach Matt would take off his shirt and shorts and pace the deck in his Speedo—a tiny flag of fabric—then jump in. The fine ribbon of muscles that traversed the length of Coach Matt's stomach reminded me of a man I'd seen in *Playboy* on the periphery, hands at his waist, backside to the camera, watching a naked woman standing in a field of tall grass.

The game started underwater, tunneling arms and legs, trying to slip beyond the shark's hands to the other side of the deep end. When Coach Matt would be the shark, my heart would beat so hard I thought it might rocket out of me. Then he tagged me beneath the water, and his hand felt so much larger and stronger than it did in real life. Underwater we seemed equals; and in my head I thought that the possibility existed.

Around this time, I began babysitting for a seven-month-old girl whose mother worked in an office during the day and sold Tupperware at night. She would pick me up on Wednesday nights in her Pontiac Grand Prix with crumpled wads of paper and gum wrappers strewn about the floor, an overly sweet air freshener swinging back and forth from the rearview mirror as the baby—Ashley—cooed in the safe cup of her car seat. They lived in one of the brown brick apartment buildings on the north end of town. Each of the units had miniature concrete patios, some of which held domed barbeque grills or pots of geraniums that had gone papery in the summer's heat. I'd help Ashley's mom carry in groceries or her briefcase while she scooped Ashley into her arms and led me up to their second-floor apartment with its shag orange carpet.

After Ashley was in bed and quiet, I'd go through all the channels on cable and then sort through the kitchen. I liked to look at the boxes of cereal and packaged food from Kellogg's and Nabisco—bags of chips and cookies my mom would never buy and I would never allow myself to eat. Dirty dishes piled the sink, toast crumbs speckled the counter—all of it so different from my mother's vinegar-scrubbed floors and spotless Formica.

One night I cracked the door to Ashley's room and checked to make sure she was still asleep. With two hours yet to go until her mom returned, I was drawn to her parents' bedroom.

The door was wide open; a small lamp glowed from the dresser top, the drawers stood open in various states—and against my better judgment, I took hold of one and tugged it further. Inside was an entire drawer of silky bras and panties, a lace corset like what Madonna wore in the "Like a Virgin," video, only the one in my hands was a soft, buttery shade. My own mother wore plain cotton bras and white panties that covered every inch. Did Ashley's mother wear slinky slippery items beneath her prim skirts and blouses?

I lifted the lingerie and held them against my own mostly flat chest. And as I did so I sensed how someday, not far off, such decisions about what I wore under my clothes might be mine as well. I imagined Coach Matt seeing me in such a flimsy material and giving me the look—the deep stare I'd felt from other men. Then he would hug me? Kiss me? I couldn't see anything beyond him looking at me with desire.

The final swim meet of the season was the Lansing B-Meet, a two-day competition hosted by our team at the outdoor pool. Considering my obsession with Coach Matt, the competition took on a different meaning. While I wanted to do well, I was more focused on the fact it would be one of the last times I'd see Coach Matt before he returned to college. I had the sense he understood something about me that my parents and friends did not and once I had this knowledge, everything else would click into place.

The day of the meet was late July and impossibly hot. Coach Matt strode the deck in shorts and a collared shirt. He looked more like an adult except for his mirrored aviator sunglasses and the thick application of pink Zinka sunscreen over his nose. I'd seen the colored sunscreen advertised in magazines and on TV commercials, but I hadn't seen anyone wearing Zinka until now.

My friend Lily and I found his pink sun-screened nose hilarious, laughing and calling him "Zinka," when he was within earshot. We couldn't keep ourselves from cracking up. A grown man with a pink nose? Surely he heard us. With every utterance we became further emboldened.

Laughing was easier than thinking about the fact that summer swim team would soon end. I consoled myself by imagining that maybe Coach Matt would stick around. But that wouldn't work, either. Soon I would be on the high school team swimming for some other coach.

But I had two events ahead of me: The 100-breaststroke and the 200-IM, an event where swimmers completed two lengths of every stroke, beginning with butterfly. I never enjoyed competitions and this one felt particularly fraught. I couldn't let Coach Matt see me fail.

The pool area was crowded with parents assisting with meet logistics from running the bullpen to keeping the concession area stocked with bananas and ice-cold cans of Pepsi. My dad worked the kyroscope, a computer system that automatically recorded the swimmers' times. He sat beneath a canopy reviewing printed read-outs of times from each heat. Mom was a stroke judge. She marched alongside the pool in white slacks and a polo shirt, making sure swimmers didn't take any illegal strokes during their races. I was embarrassed when she waved at me from the other end of the pool and offered her the smallest of gestures in return.

With just moments before my first event, I whipped my arms in circles, shaking out my legs, and then noticed the fat wiggling on them and stopped. All summer I had been thinking of Coach Matt, applying his strategies to improve my strokes, but today was one of the few times he would see me compete against other girls my age. A lump nested in my throat.

Standing on the edge of the starting block, I crouched at the ready. When the starter said, "Swimmers, take your mark," I tipped closer to my toes, cocked my arms back, and at the pop of the gun, dove into the pool.

I did what I'd been training to do: I kept my head tucked for butterfly and did three flutter kicks as I swung my arms forward and above the water. I kept going and when I hit the wall of the 50-meter pool, I pushed onto my back for backstroke. With my face out of the water, I could see the splash from the swimmers on either side of me, which meant only one thing: I was not winning.

Panic shot through me. I ordered my arms to churn with more speed. Flags overhead signaled the lane's end. I counted my strokes— one, two, three—put one arm out behind me and flipped onto my stomach for breaststroke—and discovered a surge of energy. I pushed my arms forward then swept them back in rotation, whipping my legs out in a similar movement. The crowd cheered from lawn chairs set around the pool's perimeter. Somewhere Coach Matt yelled for me as well, only I couldn't think too much about it. Now I simply needed to finish as strong as possible.

Finally, I slammed my hand into the wall and planted my feet. Chest heaving, I became aware of myself yet again. I pulled off my cap, dunked my head, and drew a slick hand over my hair. I placed my hands on the deck and pulled myself out of the pool, then headed toward Coach Matt.

"Nice job," he said. He put a hand on my shoulder and shook it.

In that instant, he seemed like any other coach I'd had, and a goofy grin spread across my face; I relished the praise of his touch.

"Thanks," I said, smiling. In the reflection of his mirrored aviator sunglasses, I saw tiny dual images of me tan and wet and panting. Even if I hadn't won, I felt strong standing there, the reflection of me momentarily part of him.

At the end of the meet, everyone pitched in to clean up. We reeled in the lane lines, took down the flags and hoisted the touch pads from the end of the pool. I still wore my swimsuit and moved about with a towel around my waist. Finally, much of the meet had been packed up and Madonna's "Open Your Heart" played from overhead speakers. A bunch of younger swimmers started pushing each other into the pool, some already dressed.

The sun strode high, shattered the water's surface into tiny pieces of glass. High school classes would start in a few weeks, but now Madonna was singing, "If you gave me half a chance you'd see my desire burning inside of me."

As Coach Matt walked by, the excitement of the meet finally over, our giddiness contagious, Lily and I teased "Zinka! Zinka!" It seemed like summer would never end, that it might go on and on in our singsong voices, where an attractive college student could be our swim coach and we could tease him like a peer.

And then I felt Coach Matt's hands on my shoulders. When I started to turn, I realized he was pulling me into the pool with him, the two of us falling sideways into the water. The slap of our splash combined. And then, as if in a dream: I was underwater with Coach Matt.

Even though I'd spent most of the summer in this very pool, nothing about the moment felt familiar. I eased to standing, water hitting me mid-stomach. Coach Matt remained behind me. I was conscious of my body, yet unsure what to do with it. He grew closer and I stilled. He didn't talk but I felt him there. I had arms and legs, a head and face. Everything felt obvious and unnatural, as if each limb were painted neon. Coach Matt positioned himself nearer and placed his hands on the tops of my arms. Mouth too dry to swallow. I stiffened. The towel I'd had wrapped around my waist ghosted off between us.

I might have laughed, unsure of what to do. There wasn't time to think. Coach Matt kept his hands on me and tipped me sideways beneath the water, then brought me up for air. He pushed me back down again like the motions that went with the song about the little teapot, only he moved faster and faster. I had to gulp air each time he drew me upright before he pushed me back down again. He steered me through the pool this way, held me close.

Chlorine tanning oil laughter Madonna sunlight sky cannonballs swim coach.

He never spoke to me, but gasping for air, I felt it. Hard at my backside. Part of him pressed fiercely against me. I didn't yet have a name for it but I knew. It had to do with boys and sex and babies, and despite my dreams of Coach Matt's affection, I was frightened. I did not know what I wanted but I did not want this. I felt an uprising inside myself, in the whole bitter world, my eyes opened to everything.

I panicked, started coughing, and he let me go. I hunched, drifted away toward the ladder; I was embarrassed by my youth and skin and body—by me.

I heaved myself out of the pool, kept my eyes on the deck as I searched for my towel then leaned over, fished it out of the pool and wrung it out like my entire life depended on it. Out of the water, I trembled. I walked with hollow legs as if I'd been emptied of whatever had filled me before. I looked around to see if anyone witnessed what had just occurred. I wasn't sure what to do. Everything felt wrong, like I had just made a mistake that would haunt me forever.

After the swim meet, the summer would piddle away. I'd watch soap operas with my sister, all of it boring and colorless. Coach Matt would return to college in Kentucky where he had his own swim coach and practice to attend. I would go over and over the moment in my head. The ending would remain the same: his hard knob poked me while the water and his grip entrapped.

In the distant future, when a college boyfriend would hold me down in his apartment bedroom, I'd discover that panic again. And later, I'd understand how a story I told myself about myself exposed me to what I wasn't prepared to live. I was fourteen years old; I wasn't yet ready for what I thought I desired. Someday I would be.

But now—on the other side of the pool—adults filled totes and sealed boxes of supplies that would be kept in storage until next year's meet. I kept my eyes on them, taking in these rote actions. My own parents heaved boxes into the open trunk of our car. Mom still wore the white polo and slacks along with moony sunglasses that took up half of her face. Every so often she stopped and ran a hand underneath the back of her hair, the hand that when I was sick she drew to my forehead to check for a fever.

After closing the trunk of the car, she said something to my dad, and he raised his hands palms up, meaning *I don't know.* They'd promised earlier we'd go out that night to Aurelio's for pizza and I thought of the five of us together over the dark wood table, an endless pitcher of root beer, Dad making a joke about something or someone, all of us relieved for the day to be over, the salty cheese, ice spinning in my glass after I took a long drink, the waitresses in their red aprons and the suckers they'd leave on the table after Dad paid the bill.

# ON THE VERGE OF BEING

We want boyfriends. We dream about Rob Lowe, Simon Le Bon from Duran Duran, Frisco on *General Hospital*, Judd Nelson. Their glossy pictures paint our locker doors and insides of our pencil cases. We send them letters, write stories crouched together in the school parking lot after classes in which each of us is alone in the dark with our idol. We slap one another on the arm, murmur, "Whatcha gonna do with them once the lights are out?" Eighth graders, we erupt into fits of laughter.

We would date the boys in our class at St. Ann's if they were datable, but Jack is taken and Mike is only cute because he's a new student and from the public school. Other boys shoot spit wads and play *Dungeons and Dragons*. Even though we're not attracted to these boys, we try to get them to notice us. We nod our heads when they talk to us, cover our mouths when we giggle, ask them questions about their basketball team. We want these boys to skate with us during "couples only" at the school skating party. In folded papers, we ask them if they will skate with our friends. Sometimes they answer. Other times they crumple the paper into a ball, aim it at a friend across the room, and let it fly.

I diet. Bran cereal and a glass of orange juice for breakfast. For lunch, a Tupperware filled with lettuce leaves, a few strips of fat-free turkey and salad dressing, an apple. I almost throw up every day when I open the container; the limp leaves pressed under oil warm from my locker. More than a boyfriend, I want to be wanted.

During school lunch, I touch my side where ribs pulse skin. They make me proud, remind me of the progress I've made. I force myself to lift a forkful of lettuce. For now, this is my secret. Dinner consists of half of everything. Fridays are the best. I allow myself half a sandwich for lunch and a slice of pizza for dinner. Sharp fisted pains bully the pit of my stomach; the hunger accompanying each day proves my toughness—that I'll win.

My younger sister Beth is in the sixth grade. A dancer, her limbs are sturdy and sinewy. The bow of her collarbone arches gracefully, her neck long and slender. She holds her head with sureness, steps with fluidity. She makes honor roll each quarter while completing her homework on the couch in front of the TV. Her teachers say she is a pleasure to have in class, that she is gifted. I bite my nails while working at my desk for hours each night stumbling over fractions and decimals, percents and positive integers. There are faceless bones to memorize for science and boldface words for history. The teacher's handwritten comments on my report card say I need to work on my study habits, that I do not follow directions, and that I should smile more.

We practice walking during recess: heads high, hips swishing. On the playground we wear our Oxford collars up, hike our plaid skirts higher, then pull them back down when the bell rings. We don't say it out loud, but we envy Anna's chest, two giant hills she cannot disguise under sweater vests or cabled cardigans. The boys make up songs about her and snap her bra more than ours. We worry our breasts will not grow.

At school, we pass around a rumpled copy of Judy Blume's *Forever*. She became our surrogate mother, teaching us everything about our bodies from masturbation to sex, menstruation to dating. Blume wrote *Forever* after her daughter requested a story where "two nice kids have sex and don't die." In our school, sex education class consisted of an hour-long discussion of male and female body parts by the school nurse, or a film strip with the science teacher, which ended with our teacher asking: "Are there any questions?"

Yes, we had questions—many, many questions, but we weren't about to ask them.

The books discussed the things our parents and teachers were too embarrassed to mention such as Michael naming his penis Ralph and Katherine and Michael dry humping with their clothes still on.

We believe we will be madly in love when we have sex. We are Catholic, so we won't have affairs like in the book, but we have faith it is okay to have sex before marriage as long as we're in love or engaged. We figure we'll marry our first loves, like our parents. This probably won't be any of the boys from our class, but we can't be certain.

Even though *Forever* explains where he puts his mouth on her, where she holds him, we're still confused on how "it" fits inside her. The thought of having kids is even more frightening. We squirm, scrunch our faces, and groan at the mention of labor. Right now, we're glad to be thirteen.

Every night behind a locked door, I lie flat on my bedroom floor and work my inner thigh muscles. Feet and neck just off the ground, fingertips on stomach, I kick my legs out until my pointed toes touch. I turn the radio loud and Whitney or Cyndi pushes me forward. After a song or two I check my progress in the floor-length mirror on the back of my door. Standing straight, I press ankles together and measure the distance between the inner thighs. They are not allowed to touch by two inches—my goal is to increase the gap by two and one-half inches. I pull the mini-ruler from my desk drawer, align feet against each other. One ankle bone abutting the other. A two-inch space exists between the uppermost thighs.

I praise my diligence.

In the kitchen I overhear them congratulate Beth; she has been invited to join a prestigious ballet troupe. Her teacher also wants her to try out for *The Nutcracker* in Chicago; she thinks Beth has a good chance at Clara's role. Beth tells them this while soaking her bloody toes in a bucket next to the kitchen table where Mom and Dad sit. She wears the black leotard from practice with the cut-out back. Mom calls Beth her little ballerina. She has her talent; I am developing mine.

We make slam books, pass them around in class. The books consist of a number of stapled sheets of looseleaf. Each paper posts a question at the top. The first page asks for full names, favorite foods, all-time favorite movie, and then they grow more interesting, demanding our secret love interest, the boy in our class we think has the sexiest eyes, the rock star we'd consider going to second base with. We try to protect them from the boys; a few immature ones always try to intercept a book while it's being delivered. When they wrestle the books out of our hands we yell, tell our teacher, Ms. Neely, and then they throw our paper books back at us, tell us we're dorks.

At home, I use our play typewriter to write letters to my crush, Jason. I've liked him since fifth grade. I can't type, so I hit return several times to position the carriage and my few sentences in the middle of the page. Typing takes work, so while my brother Michael eats Cheez-Its after swim practice and my sister watches TV, I huddle over the typewriter and tell Jason that I think he is nice, that I hope we can be friends. I end: Guess who?

His desk is near mine and if our carpool brings us to school early, I will drop a pen or folder near his desk, bend down to grab it, then stuff the envelope with its sealed letter between his books. My desk is close enough that I can watch Jason. "What the—?" he said the first time he discovered my note. I pretended to read a book, but kept sight on him out of the corner of my eye. The secret thoughts I'd been carrying around for years were now in his hands.

I dream of lemon drop cookies, thick berry shakes, Ritz crackers, Cheetos, Hershey bars with almonds. I sit in a padded chair, slowly dropping Oreos into my mouth, one after the other. Not a crumb falls, the creamy filling melts on my tongue, the chocolately cookie becomes gummy on the roof of my mouth, stuck in my teeth, the sugar sweetness waning. I weigh myself every morning. If the scale edges past 100, I am only allowed liquids for the day. No starches, definitely not bread with its yeasty heaviness.

I find Beth one afternoon bending and clapping with an exercise show. I burst past her, punch off the TV, then push her on the couch. Thinness is my talent, and I'll defend it to the end. She bites my hand, I pull her hair; I'm stronger, I can still pin her down, hold her arms above her head. She calls me a jerk, an idiot, and a cow. At that, I punch her arm, hard, leave her hunched and crying. Within minutes she's on the phone calling Mom at work. She doesn't understand, none of them do. She already has lithe legs, hips gently swooped— her thighs are slight. Beth's grades and knowledge impress. She has a multitude of compliments to play with; I have only one that hangs loosely, dangles precariously. These protruding bones, this hunger, becomes evidence.

We think Ms. Neely must be the ugliest woman alive. Once a nun, she now wears plain-colored polyester pants, her saddlebag hips coming and going, jelly skin and belly bulges. Black moles on her face sprout hair. We don't say it aloud, but we fear growing up and growing out. We want to wear bikinis forever, toss our hair back and laugh at jokes, coat our lips with colored wands. We know how to be girls; we know what's expected of us; we cannot respect the older women who forget their bodies and haunt our futures.

After school, in a moment of weakness, I eat a homemade chocolate chip cookie; it's warm and sticky, chocolate smears my fingers and I lick each one clean. I pop the last bite into my mouth and panic— what have I done? I turn the radio on in my room and start jumping jacks, push-ups, inner thigh exercises, deep knee bends, stretches, I beg it, "Please leave!" I apologize to myself, promise it won't happen again.

On the weekends, Beth's teachers have arranged for her to take a class for gifted students at the junior college. Dad wakes early to drive her. As a tinge of light flirts the blinds, Mom prepares blueberry pancakes, the griddle sizzling with fat, the smell of hotcakes wafting to where I remain cloaked under blankets. They are talking about the future. Dad wants her to be a doctor and offers to arrange for Beth to shadow a female physician at Suburban Hospital. Dad says, "Just think about all the things you'll be able to do with that kind of money, that kind of position." Mom reminds her she can do anything with her grades and motivation—the sky's the limit.

Meanwhile, Dad sits with me at the kitchen table at night and writes mixed fractions with a black ballpoint pen on a legal pad. I am supposed to make the fractions whole. I pause, pencil poised over the problem. He slams his fist at my slowness, points out the steps to follow. My fingers fall slack, unmoving, unable to join together and hold the pencil. It slips from my fingers. "Tell me what you can't see. What's so difficult here?" *I can't see a thing*, I think. Instead, I nod my head in recognition. He thinks I've finally caught on, moves to the next fraction. It's difficult to focus, and grainy light passes before my eyes. I imagine they are numbers speeding past, unable to be seized.

We want to be marine biologists, lawyers, rock stars, actresses, and nurses. We want to live in Europe and California where famous people walk the streets and you can run into Michael J. Fox in the cereal aisle of the grocery store. We want to own horses in our backyards, kittens and old dogs. We want a koala bear to wrap its arms and legs around us wherever we go.

Mom takes me to the doctor because my periods have stopped. They take my blood pressure, listen to my heart. The diagnosis: low body fat. They place me on a two-thousand-calorie diet. The doctor reminds me that I am a growing girl—boys and girls need fat for their bodies to run effectively. Mom looks serious, steely-eyed. He says, "Don't you want to have a baby someday?"

Mom answers for me, "Of course she does."

This is how they think it will be: I will have arms full of babies, Beth will make a torrent of money as a physician. She will be able to come and go as she pleases while I'll be weighted by sticky hands clawing my knees.

I will be the beautiful one. I will wear sequined ball gowns, step out of sleek limousines, my manicured hand on the lintless jacket of a handsome man. Everyone will look. They'll eye the cut of my hair, the lean fit of my dress. They will be amazed at how tall I stand, how perfectly ordered.

I have plans too.

Over dinner, Dad asks what we did that day. Mom says I'm having female problems, nothing to fear. Dad lifts a forkful of meat and says, "It's always one thing or another with you women." I smile, agree. Mom watches me eat dinner. She has made gravy, vegetables swimming in butter, oily red meat runny with juices. She forces me to remain at the table until my plate is clean. She sits across from me,

arms folded, expects me to swallow the last few forkfuls. Dad is waiting to work on math, Mom says not until I finish eating. "Let her do
what she wants," he says. *Yeah, Mom*, I think. His words hang overhead while I stare at the heaping plate.

Beth has started to take salads for lunch; she hides this from
Mom. I see her throw the lunch Mom has made in her bookbag,
sneak some lettuce into a container, slip this into a new brown paper
bag. She thinks she can beat me at this as well.

We roll our eyes when we talk about our parents. We think they're
clueless, that we surprised them altogether, that they never imagined
the tiny bundles they brought back from the hospital would grow
into small people. "I can't believe how my mom dresses. I wish she
could at least wear better jeans," says one of my friends.

"I'd be okay if for once they took us to play mini-golf on Saturday. Instead, all they do is complain about how much it costs,"
adds another. All of us wish that for a moment they could try and
understand.

For the present, Mom makes sandwiches for me to take to school.
They are soft with mayonnaise and double slices of cheese. It's on
her mind now; she'll soon forget this latest vow. I count each bite,
teeth sinking into gluey bread, pink meat. Mom threatens to talk to
my teacher if I don't eat my sandwich. I manage four bites. I fold the
sandwich in a sheet of looseleaf, prepare to show it to my teacher
if she stops to check on me. I eat my apple, hold macaroons in one
hand. I squint at my reflection on my desktop. Lunch period lasts
too long.

It's against school policy to wear makeup, but today I smuggle
discounted makeup to class in my purse. After the lunch bell, we
huddle around the bathroom mirror, pass tubes of hot-pink lipstick
and sparkly shadows. We try everything. We borrow mascara from
each other, coat our lashes two or three times. I pull out a mini can

of aerosol hair spray, cement the rolls of bangs half-concealing my eyes, then scurry to class. We know Ms. Neely will make us wash our eyes after she inspects our faces from her post outside the classroom door; it won't be like this in a few months. I can't wait for high school. Some of us will have boy-girl parties. We'll play Spin the Bottle. Someone will sneak in a golden bottle of liquor, the cap crusty; it will burn my throat, make me sputter and cough, warm my belly. I'll feel giggly, daring, bold. I'll speak loudly here, for the first time, and the others will listen. When we hear adult shoes on the stairs we'll roll the bottle under the couch, keep our faces straight, tell our parents we're having a great time.

# COTTON

I was ten when I took Dad's hand and placed it on top of my undershirt to feel the bump. "Maybe I broke a rib or something?" I asked. Outside, bugs flicked their bodies against the window screen. He swallowed, didn't meet my eyes. I stood still, waited. It was bedtime but I thought someone needed to know and Mom was busy putting away the dinner dishes. The curtains wafted in the nighttime air.

"Do you feel it?" I asked, holding his wrist and moving the closed paddle of his hand around the hard round mass on my chest, white cotton bunching. Perhaps something had begun to grow at the wrong angle. Maybe I was dying.

Orange light flooded the alley between the apartments and our backyard. "Go to bed," Mom said from the other side of the kitchen.

I crossed my arms and went to my bedroom.

I wondered if I would have to see our pediatrician, Dr. Angeles. He had a missing pinkie finger that looked like a headless puppet that refused to bend.

I lay in bed with a hand on my chest and pushed the matter around. It was firm and round as a silver dollar, but Mom and Dad hadn't seemed concerned. Truth is, if I did have some incurable disease—the first of its kind—I didn't know how they would feel.

Trembling, I wondered if this meant something else altogether.

* * *

Mom's breasts were two large pendulous things that she kept batted down beneath heavy white bras with two and three clasps. The straps made divots on her skin, created half-moons on her back, a faint shadow of red that remained even after she unfastened her bra and her flesh sprung free. I learned not to stare; only this was impossible when we camped at Three Braves, where we spent most summer weekends.

My sister and I stood in the campground bathhouse in our flip-flops and the homemade cover-ups Mom had stitched from bath towels, waiting for a shower to vacate. When the handicapped stall was free, Mom insisted we take it.

After locking the stall door, Mom unpacked her denim bag. Shampoo and conditioner, soap in an orange plastic caddy, Shower-to-Shower talc. She instructed us to undress. We don't have all day, she said.

In the shower, my sister and I stood naked while Mom leaned over us in her bra and underwear. She pressed the nozzle, and it honked to life with a fine spray. After undressing, Mom joined us, pushing us closer to the nozzle. Droplets formed on Beth's head and Mom's hands ground the water into my sister's scalp. The smell of campfire and lake water rose around us.

The flesh on Mom's chest and belly wiggled, the ends of her breasts like two cocoa-colored eyeballs. She arranged us beneath the mist and then her hands opened the folds of my body to the water. Somehow, I knew this was what it meant to be a good girl, to stand beneath a single showerhead with my younger sister and mom, to be scrubbed clean.

\* \* \*

In *Excalibur*, the woman rises bare-chested from the water. In *Flashdance*, Alex works as a dancer and strips to make extra money. It's impossible to recall the first time I saw a bare chest in a movie. Instead, they blur together—*Little Darlings, Airplane!, Animal House.* There is always a scene with a topless woman, breasts flapping. Mom uses an afghan to cover the heads of my sister and me when these scenes come on the screen. Our brother is older and does not have to hide from the breasts like we do.

I don't yet have breasts, but assume that the gelatinous mounds are coming. With the blanket over my head, knees pressed against my flat chest, I peer through the blanket's open knots, the heat of my face hidden.

\* \* \*

His mouth covered mine.

His name was Blake or Brandon. Something with a B. He was three years older than me and we were smashed in the back seat of his friend's sedan—six of us in all—on some nameless road in Michigan, the lake a hushed expanse behind a bayonet of trees. The sun had set hours ago and now, after hanging out at Brandon's parents' cottage, his friend drove us back to the campground where our parents sat around a campfire drinking.

The road crusted with sand and weeds, music from the speakers loud and insistent. It was my first kiss and we had gotten it out of the way hours previous; I already felt older, wiser. I knew how to tip my face and had already discovered that the best place for my hands were the bulbs of Brandon's shoulders, gaping from his tank top.

Sara sat in the front with the driver, and Tonya and her guy were at my left. Sisters, I'd known Tonya and Sara since we were seven. We swam weeknights on the local swim team and competed in races on the weekends, only they never attended Sunday meets. Their mom was very strict. She didn't believe girls should go to college or have short hair. Without talking about it, as music spun out the windows, tires spit up gravel, I knew Sara and Tonya would never let a boy do what Brandon was doing to me, only I seemed unable to stop it. His body weighted on mine like my flesh had never belonged to me and he was only now reclaiming it.

With each turn, our frames swung one way, then the other; wind-splattered hair whipped in every direction. Brandon tasted of Certs and beer.

The car's sword tips of light split the dark, made it seem as if we were soaring somewhere in space. My hands trickled over the back of Brandon's neck and I felt the gumminess of his hair gel, how it separated the strands into fat chunks, which is where my fingers were when I felt his hand beneath my shirt.

I froze.

Tonya and her guy were laughing about something. My breath caught. Brandon fastened his hand around the outside of my bra and began to push the cup in a slow circle. White breathable cotton. Mom had bought it with me from a store called Someone Special.

My face flamed. Sara and Tonya were right there. I wanted to push Brandon away. To hit reverse. But who was I to interrupt his longings?

I took shallow sips of air to keep myself from making some weird animal noise. I split my eyes, tried to see what was next.

# THE TELLING

The week of the Turnabout dance, I kept the dress on a hanger, displayed it in front of my closet like a black beacon. It was a simple black velvet cocktail dress with long sleeves and a deep V in the front and back. I'd ordered it from a catalog and when I lifted it from its box, the soft panels of the skirt unfolded like wings and the tissue paper surrounding it made a shivery sound, like a secret whispered between hands. I put all my faith in the dress, because the few times I called Gideon, reading from questions I'd jotted in advance on a piece of paper, Gideon burned through every get-to-know-you query in a matter of minutes and he never asked me anything in response. When I sauntered over to his locker clutching my books and smiling, he just looked at me as if he had no idea who I was, but then his friends would punch him in the shoulder and he would tip his head to the side as if it were too heavy. A senior, he was a year older than me and was a starter on our school basketball team. I asked him to be my date for Turnabout, a dance where the girls invited the boys, because of his height, the fact that I thought he was cute, and, most important, he didn't have a girlfriend.

The night of the dance, I wasn't sure he would arrive.

I made an appointment to get my hair done. We had a swim invitational that day, which wouldn't leave much time to get ready. Plus, I was too nervous to fix my own hair. As the stylist's fingers pulled and twisted my hair, I found myself relaxing into the beauty routine and by the time she handed me a mirror to see the back of my head, the transformation into someone beautiful had begun.

As I dressed, I listened to New Order. "How does it feel/To treat me like you do?" With each move, my fears and insecurities blurred into the background. My friends would be there and if nothing else, we would dance. Still, I worried about Gideon and how little we'd talked. I thought about creating another list of questions I could use during the drive, just like *'Teen* advised, but there wasn't time. I listened to my music, let it distract me as I put on makeup, then sat on the edge of my bed and pushed a fist through a new pair of black pantyhose, before inserting my foot and easing the material over my leg. Maybe the whole idea of asking a guy I didn't know to a dance had been a mistake.

"I know you don't know who I am, but I wondered if you wanted to go to Turnabout," I had said that January night weeks ago, standing outside the doors the boys exited after basketball practice. I squinted in the hard glare of the parking lot lights. I smiled. I'd put on blush and lip gloss. We didn't have swim practice that night, so I'd told my parents I was studying at Emily's house and would be back before ten.

Gideon mumbled "Sure," and I breathed in the winter air and blew it back, swift, even clouds rising. Even now, I feel the stiffness of his look as if he were waiting for me to criticize him. But I was shiny and peppy: I would make him like me.

"Cool! I'm Melissa!" I said, turned on my heel and forced myself not to run back to my car.

I couldn't wait to tell my friends. At that time, I believed the telling was more important than the lived experience, how seeing it unfold in another person's face, it became real.

Finally, I slipped the dress off its hanger and stepped into it. Lined in silky fabric, the dress felt like zipping myself into a small body of water. I ran a hand along the velvet bodice, the plushness powerful and enthralling.

I was in my room when the doorbell rang. Mom was away that day and I froze at the idea of Gideon chatting with Dad in his olive-green sweater with the oil stain on the chest. I hurried to our living room where Gideon stood holding a clear plastic box with a pink lily, my least favorite flower with its thick funereal scent. He held the box toward me and after what seemed like minutes, I took it, as if in doing so I was entering into some silent agreement.

I slipped the elastic over my wrist, then reached up to pin the rose boutonniere to his lapel. I hadn't stood this close to him before and felt the hot slap of my heart inside my dress. Dad picked up his camera. Usually, I smiled and showed my teeth in photos, only in the picture Dad took that night my mouth is closed, face arranged in uncertainty as if someone had not just fixed my hair but rearranged my features. I took a breath, willed myself to relax.

"Have fun, be careful!" Dad said, shutting the front door behind us.

The stairs were slicked with ice from a storm earlier that week and my nylons whooshed together; I held tight to the metal banister as Gideon marched ahead. I let myself in the passenger side. Imprisoned by the hard chill of the seat, Gideon backed out of our drive.

As we drove, I watched the neighbors' houses blur past like my own life were being shown to me on a screen. Gideon changed the radio station from classic rock to 97.9 where Steve Tyler crooned, "Janie's got a gun." Salt plunked underneath the car tires; heat blasted my black bowed pumps; I thought they might melt, but wasn't about to move them: the warmth a comfort.

The dance was held at a restaurant that doubled as a banquet hall, set back along a series of strip malls on Cicero Avenue; overhead, planes zoomed to Midway Airport. Gideon turned into the parking lot. Other friends were getting out of their cars, and we waved our tiny beaded purses at one another, complimented each other's dresses and hair. A whole group of us swooped into the hall at the same time. Heat gushed around us. No one wore a coat or jacket and we opened and closed our hands to warm them. Chaperones stood in the vestibule, welcoming us, directing us toward the ballroom with its dim lights and chandelier. The DJ stood at a table in the front of the dance floor nodding his head along to U2's "Sunday Bloody Sunday." Gideon and I entered the room together, but then we floated off in separate directions. I strolled to the buffet with friends where we filled plates with baby quiche and squares of white cheese, crackers. Across the room, Gideon stood in a clump with his basketball teammates.

We'd only exchanged a handful of words since we arrived and when "Nothing Compares 2 U" blasted from the speakers, nearly every couple flooded the dance floor and I found myself next to Gideon. I didn't want to look at him, to see the confirmation I knew would be there: He didn't want anything to do with me. The truth pierced and the air inside me further dribbled out.

As we swayed, I lifted a hand from the back of Gideon's button-down shirt to brush the velvet at my waist, smooth as a baby's skin. Beside me a girl tucked her head beneath her boyfriend's chin. I didn't have the boyfriend, but I had the dress.

When the dance was over, a whole group of us shuffled out of the hall, the crunch of taffeta and lace, the click-clack of heels. Some people were talking about an afterparty at a hotel in Harvey, and as we worked on plans, my anxieties returning, I replayed the asking.

*You mean you didn't even know him? I can't believe you! That's hilarious!*

I saw myself smiling, standing in the school parking lot saying, "You don't know me, but do you want to go to Turnabout?"

I felt a small fist of pride in my boldness, only the story wasn't enough to absorb the hollowness that permeated the inside of Gideon's car, some long-leaned thing that after the dance ended drove me to a hotel in Harvey, the one right off I-80/94. Someone rented several rooms and filled a bathtub with cans of beer and ice. One room held a keg and the guys took turns filling red tumblers, handing out foamy cups. After arriving at the hotel, I lost track of him, which relieved me in some ways. I stood in a circle with my friends from the swim team and had to tip my cup nearly all the way back before tasting beer. So many of us from the dance were jammed together in that room, sidestepping the beds. Several of the girls discarded their heels in a corner pile. I kept mine on, afraid of snagging my new nylons.

Gideon appeared. Did I seek him out, or had he come up to me, spied me from across the room, maybe ready to finally talk? *What classes do you like in school? Are you having a good time? Do you want another beer?*

The alcohol loosened the unease in my belly and I grinned at him without willing myself to do so and then it was just the two of us and we were in an altogether different place, the hotel room as quiet as a can of soup.

In that space, alone with Gideon standing in front of me, I tried to smile, but it was as if the muscles in my mouth had stopped working. Gideon leaned down and kissed me, only it was more braces than his lips and then I was falling, his hands pushing me on the bed; I put my arms around him, like the magazines instructed, the bed beneath me liquid, each kiss exposed his braces. My mouth hurt. I wanted to tell him. I drew back one time to touch my lips but then we were kissing again. Maybe it was his first? Each kiss sliced into me like a paper cut, but the dress draped me, even on the bed, and I sensed its presence, a soft circle of fabric holding me in its soothing embrace. I'd kept the box and tissue paper that the dress arrived in, pushing it beneath my bed, this place where Mom once tucked me in at night and sometimes still crept in the room before dawn to wake me. I liked to sit in my bed with the pillows stacked behind me and read or write in my journal; sometimes at night when I couldn't sleep, I'd split the blinds with my fingers and watch light skitter from my wrist to my bedroom wall, but then Gideon, he was still here, and

I was alone with him, took the shoulders of my dress in his hands and yanked it down, ripping the velvet at the V. *He's trying to take it off*, I thought, and grabbed the fabric at my chest, tried to push the ends together, to make them whole, the threads popping up as if electrified.

And then the lips and braces returned, tiny slashes that burned my face for days afterward. I let him kiss me. Hadn't I been the one to ask him? Hadn't he been the one to accept my invitation?

He ripped my dress. My beautiful dress.

Someone knocked on the door and I jumped to answer it. Welcoming the chilled blast, the smear of lights and billboards on the distant expressway. It was Eric, the boy who had given me a tin of Hershey kisses and a mixtape for my birthday freshman year.

"Why is your mouth bleeding?" he asked.

His breath rose above him as he talked and time seemed to slow. It was like he was visiting me from another country. I patted my lips and the skin around it, then looked down at my pinked palm. I crossed my arms, held myself. "I don't know," I said. My mouth hurt. I disguised the rip of my dress behind a hand.

And then it came to me: Gideon thinks I'm pretty.

Gideon slunk to the door with disheveled hair, his shirt wrinkled. He was a solid head taller than Eric. "Hey man," they shook hands, "What's up?" Standing up in the fresh air, seeing the metal door wide open, I remembered my friends. As Eric and Gideon talked, I located my shoes inside the doorway. When I bent down to slip them on, my head pounded. *Get out, get out,* I thought. Any ease I'd felt from the beer had disappeared. A numbness settled in. I heard the screech of the dress's tear again, the noise lingered, an echo of blame.

I strode away on the concrete walkway that lined the hotel perimeter, my eyes tearing in the wind. I imagined a line before me and concentrated on positioning the toes of my heels directly on it. I placed one foot then followed with the other.

Back in the room with the keg, surrounded by friends, I sipped another cup of foam.

"Where were you?" Someone asked. I gestured vaguely at the space on the other side of the door.

I slanted the cup so the bubbles ticked against the cuts on my mouth and held my other arm over my chest. When someone said something funny, I laughed. When no one was looking, I turned away.

Emily and her date blasted Pink Floyd as they drove me home. Outside my house, Emily hugged me goodbye, then got back in the car. As they drove off, tires crackling on frosted pavement, I stood beneath the trees' icy skeletons and breathed in the black night. Swift, even clouds ascending.

There was no way I was going to tell my friends what happened to me. Not Emily or anyone else from the swim team. Definitely not my mom who the next day, asked if I'd had fun. Gideon and I never spoke again and when we passed in the halls he did not look my way. When anyone brought up Turnabout, I listened to their stories, nodded and smiled, the whole time thinking of the dress in the back of my closet in its plastic shroud.

But the night after the dance, safe inside my bedroom, I was still caught between the story I wanted to tell myself and what had actually happened. When I unzipped the dress and hung it so it again stood in front of the closet door, the panels of the skirt drooped. I examined the tear. I told myself it wasn't that bad. There were splotches on the fabric where I'd spilled beer. They weren't wet, but they'd left an odd sheen, like a mirage that could only be seen if I tilted the fabric in certain light.

# MORE LIKE DAD

"Keep your eyes open," Dad says. The left one keeps pinching shut.

I am eight when I shoot my first gun. Stretched out on my stomach in our backyard, the trigger of the .22 pellet air gun nearly liquid behind my finger. I aim the front sight on the water-filled milk jug. I think of pulling the trigger and how with one quick movement I could kill. My perspiration prints the barrel. I want to wipe my hands on my shorts but worry about putting down the gun. What if I suddenly turn the gun toward my sister or Dad or myself?

I could kill someone. One wrong move and they'd be shattered, falling to the ground, blood leaking from a hole I made.

As frightened as I am, I know I need to do this so he will like me. To learn how to shoot a gun. To be more like Dad.

\* \* \*

Dad keeps his guns in the basement. Rifles are in individual padded cases that lean butt-side down along the water heater. His handguns are stacked in hard plastic cases on an adjoining metal shelf. This is where he also stores his cleaning supplies: Hoppe's gun cleaner, spray lubricant, compact brushes and pins. I never touch his guns—none of us do—but they are there—and all I have to do is fall in love with them, solve the puzzle of their beauty.

\* \* \*

*Goddamnsonofabitch* or *sonofabitch* or *whatthehelliswrongwithyou?* Dad yells when the newspaper arrives wet, the dog gets loose, Mom backs the car into the side of the garage, someone has a fever, or the sump pump fails and the basement floods. Each of his curses has a different tone, but all of them reverberate off the walls. His deep and endless rage threatens to crack the plaster, lift the roof off the house, and send it flying.

I learn to listen to the crackle of the newspaper in his hands as he turns the pages, or how hard he closes the cabinet door after getting out the bag of peanuts and a bowl, where he sits each night at the kitchen table. Sometimes he smashes the shell against his thumb, pulls apart the halves and hucks the nuts into his mouth. Other times he bashes the shell against the table, turns it into frayed bits then lifts the nuts with his fingers, whole and undisturbed.

* * *

After Dad's father died, everything changed.

Dad had been in ninth-grade geometry when he saw his brother in the doorway—and he must have known. As they stood there amid the hall of lockers, the framed paintings of Jesus and his disciples, the floors that gleamed with their reflections, my uncle told him their dad was in the hospital and doing poorly. I've seen pictures of Dad then: his too-large ears and slender form. Even then I can see how his shoulders have a way of slumping forward as if he wouldn't mind disappearing.

My grandmother had only attended school up until the fourth grade. My grandfather had been a barber. Money had always been tight, but now everyone needed to pitch in.

Dad's oldest brother took a discharge from the army. His other brother, a senior in high school, took a job bagging groceries while my dad began working as a soda jerk at Manor Drugs. My aunt and uncle moved into the Chicago two-flat where Dad and his family lived to help make ends meet and my quiet father with his too-large ears grew even quieter.

\* \* \*

As he explains that the .22 caliber is named after the diameter of the pellet, Dad loads the ammunition in the action, and then pumps the gun, pushing the pellet into the chamber. It's the same size as the graphite in a mechanical pencil. *That's pretty small*, I think. I look at the rifle in my hands. Imagine the pellet zipping through the long metal tube to the end of the gun. Other parts include the trigger, the sight, the magazine, the safety. The trigger guard remains closest to the trigger. I keep my finger clear of this until I'm ready to shoot. Even then, my stomach twists and turns. I swallow air, let it fill me with false assurance.

\* \* \*

The neighbor across the street works construction. Two houses down, Mr. Sterling fixes air conditioners and heaters. He is also my friend Rebecca's stepdad and spends weekends hunting. The head of a deer stands mounted inside the rear wall of his garage, just above the workbench. "Who are you? How dare you?" it seems to ask, glistening black eyes following me. It looks so unnatural hanging there. Each fall, I watch Mr. Sterling drive off in his pickup dressed in camouflage. One of those times he'd gone off and shot a deer, then paid someone to cut off its head, hang it right here.

Sometimes Rebecca and her family share dinner with friends from their church. I imagined the kids huddled at one end of the table, joking. The parents, more subdued, would be deep in conversation. We didn't have close family friends like that. Grandma told us how, as a boy, Dad promised everyone that when he was older, he would have a house surrounded by a fence so tall no one would be able to get in.

Dad used to say, "I could have been someone."

"You *are* someone," I'd say. And later I'd think, *If you aren't someone, then who am I?*

\* \* \*

My sister and I call Dad a lion tamer behind his back. I still hear the click of his belt as he undoes it, the whistling sound as it slides it out from the loops of his Levis. We all know to run and hide. We scramble beneath the beds or inside a closet. Sometimes I hide beneath the twin beds my sister and I push together and smoosh myself against the wall. From there I watch my dad on his hands and knees snake the belt back and forth as he tries to reach my sister. The thick leather thwomps the carpet. Under the cobwebbed shadows, she looks far away. I reach a hand out, try to pull her closer. At least, that's what I like to think I did.

\* \* \*

Sometime in the early 1980s, Dad buys a small used motorboat. One Saturday afternoon after we'd spent the day on Cedar Lake, we wade with our boat near the public entrance ramp and watch as a shirtless guy with a cigarette tries to excavate the back end of his car from the lake. With time, more boaters accrue there, all of them holding tight to their bobbing boats while the Buick's tires screech and blue plumes rise. Dad joins a group of men who gather thigh-deep in the water, put their hands on the backside of the car and push it while the driver steers the car out of the lake, one flip-flopped foot hanging out the open door.

Finally, it is our turn. Dad backs the trailer down the ramp. When the water rolls to the halfway mark of the trailer's tires, we yell for him to stop. Dad shifts the car into park, gets out to check the water's level. Too shallow and the motor would scrape the bottom. Too deep and we'd be in the same position as the man with the Buick, unable to get our car out of the lake.

"It's too deep!" he barks, shaking his head and getting back into the car. Everything inside me jostles like the current roping the edges of the lake. I stare at the line of water in the middle of the tires. It is exactly where he'd told us it should be.

My fingers go gummy, stop working.

We scamper to the side as Dad secures the hook to the boat's cleat and starts cranking it onto the trailer. He slaps the pin in place, then throws himself into the car and drives up the ramp, waiting in the parking lot with the hazards on.

We scramble barefoot through the gravel, our feet chalked white.

Dad doesn't talk to us until we are past the blinking stop sign in front of the drugstore, heading back home, and slowly ascending the hill past the squat homes with their insides out—a rack of clothes, bundles of wood for sale, turned over tricycles and rusty scooters. Dad punches the steering wheel in rhythm with his words. "You. Have. Got. To. Know. How. To. Get. That. Boat. Out. Of. The. Water."

All the windows are down. I sit in the backseat alongside my sister, the hot breeze snapping my sunburned cheeks. My brother is in front. I wear a white terrycloth cover-up over my suit and the backs of my legs stick to the vinyl. I watch the speedometer climb as the car flattens out. Thick shrubs and mulberry trees with crescent-shaped pods crowd the roadside.

When he speaks next, his voice sounds normal. Calm. He holds the steering wheel on either side, his olive skin dark from the sun. "If I'm not here tomorrow, you've got to know how to take care of the boat."

My heart jolts. I look at my sister playing with the hem of her cover-up. I am hot with panic. Even though I never get sick in the car, I worry this time I might. Everything inside me churns.

*Dad is dying*, I think. *Tomorrow he might not be here.*

\* \* \*

My report card is peppered with Cs. Teachers say I don't pay attention and that I could benefit from a review of basic math. But that's
not everything: I don't win races in the pool or get the volleyball over
the net.

I tell myself he yells because of me.

I clean the bathroom, babysit for the neighbors' kids, set the table
and make the salad. When Mom goes to work, I open the box of
frozen fried chicken and drop the gnarled blocks onto the 9×13-inch
baking pan and push this into a 350-degree oven. I'm simply doing
what I've been told, only there is more to it: If I swim faster, study
harder, pick up my room without being told, I can heal the rusted
fury inside him.

\* \* \*

Years later, I am a parent, preparing to stain our backyard fence with
my own two daughters. It hasn't been done in ages. Soft green moss
covers some of the cedar boards. The first step is to power wash, only
I can't get the dang rental to turn over. Both of my daughters stand
on opposite sides of me spraying the wood with a bleach mixture. I
open and close the choke and pull the cord for the umpteenth time
without success when Jolie stops to ask me a question.

"I don't know!" I yell, glaring at her. The heat from my reaction
rushes to the tips of my fingers, trickles up the back of my neck,
steels my jaw.

She's wearing a sun hat with a wide brim, one my husband and I
bought her two years ago for canoeing; it's likely the last year it will
fit. Her eyes, almond-shaped and brown, look at the ground. Her
shoulders sink and her mouth, where she once fed from my breast,
clenches like a piece of rotted fruit. She mumbles that she is sorry.

I stand there with the righteousness of my anger, the stupid nozzle of the power washer weighing my hand. "I'm sorry. I'm sorry I yelled," I say, walking over to her.

"It's okay," she says.

"I just want to get this started before Dad gets home," I say, realizing how stupid this sounds.

"I understand."

The blow of my words lingers. A breeze kicks up. Guilt yokes my neck.

\* \* \*

It isn't easy to hit a target. Sometimes the shooter will flinch when they pull the trigger, preparing for kickback, or the wind can force a bullet to drift. Sometimes instead of rotating in a circle, a pellet from an air rifle will tumble like a person might tumble head over feet, causing the pellet to drop during flight. The pellet hits the target sideways, leaving a keyhole-shaped impression.

When I am ten, my brother and I are invited to spend the afternoon with our friends from the swim team, Nina and Trevor William. Mom has told me previously that Mr. William has lost his job, but I'm not sure what that means. Dad works as a pharmacist. Mom is a nurse. They've changed jobs but they've never lost them. Still, the Williams have an above-ground pool that takes up most of their backyard. Trevor is a year older than my brother. Nina is a year younger than me. We aren't as close as other teammates from the swim team, but she also has a stuffed Snoopy and a whole group of us spend time between events at meets dressing our Snoopy dolls and acting out scenes.

Mom drops my brother and me over at the Williams house after swim practice. They live in the oldest part of Lansing—brick bungalows with peaked roofs and tiny backyards with chain-link fences. The four of us spend the whole afternoon bopping in the water, jogging in the same direction to make a whirlpool, then yelling "Stop!" and lifting our feet, letting the current carry us.

Nina and I share an inflatable raft and our brothers slip underwater and try to flip our boat. Mrs. William, a soft-voiced woman whose skin is as creamy as yogurt, serves us Ritz crackers with squirty cheese and slices of hot dogs. The crackers are salty and fresh, snapping in two as I bite them. We eat while leaning over the side of the pool, water tapping our sides. We take turns using the nozzle to make elaborate swirls with the cheese. Afterward, Nina and I wrap towels around our midsections and she takes me to her attic bedroom. The ceiling slants on two sides. A window looks out into the pool where our brothers float on the raft we vacated.

Nina has two cases full of Barbie clothes and we spend the rest of the afternoon dressing Barbies for their own pool party as our swimsuits dry and the air conditioner blitzes us with a steady stream.

We play in the pool and change Barbies' outfits, and other than setting out the snack when we are outside, I don't see Mr. or Mrs. William. It's like Trevor and Nina live alone in this house with their toys and their own pool. No one bosses them around. No one gets angry. When Mom comes to pick us up, I don't want to leave.

Marcia nominated Mr. Brady for Father of the Year. She missed curfew in order to make the magazine's deadline and Mr. Brady grounded her.

Tony Micelli, a former Major League Baseball player, and his daughter Sam, moved from Brooklyn to Connecticut where the schools were better and he could work as a live-in housekeeper for Angela Bower, a divorced ad executive and her son.

The girls on *One Day at a Time* might as well not have had a dad; at least he never appeared on the show. They moved to Indianapolis after their mom divorced and befriended Dwayne, the apartment's maintenance man. He stopped over to unclog a drain or check the furnace, but also to have a slice of coffee cake. You wondered what it was like living in an apartment with just your mom and sister.

Did you really need a dad?

\* \* \*

Rebecca and I play Little House on the Prairie in her backyard. From where we stand inside the pioneer-style playhouse, with its split wood and open-air windows, I can hear her stepdad, Mr. Sterling, working on his van. Loud pops of grated metal buzz on and off.

We take turns being Laura and Ma. It's fun to be Laura, since she's the same age as us, but Ma gets to tell Laura what chores to do.

Even in the cold of November, I submerge my hands in the washtub we've filled with water. The skin flushes red but I don't lift them. We don't have soap, so I try to make up for it by making my hands extra wet. Plus, we're worried. There isn't enough money for eggs or flour and we don't have enough meat to get us through winter. We don't know what to do and hope Pa comes back soon from town with the other men, before the storm strikes and we are left alone.

\* \* \*

When we shoot, Dad fills gallon jugs with water and sets them in the grass alongside the garage. Sometimes he takes empty soup cans, peels off the labels, and stacks them in a triangle. But I much prefer the jugs with their faint milky opalescence, the satisfaction of the pellet's pop, water jousting in a sure sprig. I stretch out in the grass on my elbows with my legs flat behind me. Dad reconfigures my grip or rearranges the stock of the pellet rifle. Even now I see its glossy wood twinkling in the late-day sun. "No, not like that," he'd say. "Hold it like this." Only his directions were comely and warm, unlike how it felt when I hunched over my math book at the kitchen table and he tried to help me with homework. I feel his delight as he squats beside me, touches my arms or hands.

The places he touches buzz with that gesture.

I aim the barrel; line up the open sight with the center of the jug. My pointer finger, already on the trigger, pulls back. The plastic jug plinks, water erupts in a slender fountain. Dad pats me on the back, "Nice job, kid. Nice job."

\* \* \*

I was certain that if I tried hard enough, I might release Dad from his anger, that near-constant purse of his mouth. In the swimming pool, on the gymnastics mat, in the voices of my coaches and teachers— certainly at some point I'd win and then those achievements would be enough to quell his unease. It was up to me to deliver Dad from his pain, like he was still that fourteen-year-old boy yanked out of geometry to learn his father was in the hospital dying. All that rage still flooded his veins and I would be the one to bleed it out of him, just like Dr. Baker might have done to Mary Ingalls when she got scarlet fever.

And if I failed? Then Dad would die without its release. All dads die.

\* \* \*

"How did he die?" Someone asks.

"He shot himself," says Mom. "In the garage."

Mom pats my back after she tells us, and the blood inside me slows to a trickle.

Dad rubs his eyes. Dinner has been put away. I trace the outline of a woodland mushroom on the plastic tablecloth; it feels both slippery and cool to the touch. Our dog J.R. sleeps on a scrap of green carpet in the kitchen corner, his breathing a soft purr. I try to pull together every detail of Mr. William, to make him into Nina and Trevor's father. He had a thick mustache and I'd never seen him dressed in anything other than a concert T-shirt.

I see the swimming pool in their backyard, and how the water spun after we'd made our whirlpool. The garage was just off to the side, one window facing the pool. And now I hear a shot, not unlike the shots we'd fired in our own backyard.

Dad gets up from the table and goes into the other room. This is all new to me. Someone could choose to kill themselves?

I have only attended Aunt Mary's wake and funeral. Her wrinkles painted smooth; the mound of her hands held a rosary on her chest. Death, I had thought, was reserved for the elderly after illness.

Mr. William was Trevor and Nina's dad.

I see the boxes of Barbie clothes in Nina's room, the tiny Barbie chair and table that stands crooked on the shag carpet. The room is dim—dimmer than I recall—and now I hear the shot followed by a scream.

\* \* \*

Sometimes I bark when my daughters ask me a question and I'm trying to figure something on my computer. The red heat of irritation floods me followed by the release: quick and sweet. Within seconds, I want to take those words and stuff them back inside my mouth, swallow them whole. I want to stop whatever I'm doing, take their hands and ask them to tell me something—anything. I want to watch their faces and listen to their voices. But the compulsion to yell, to lash out, is automatic. I wait for them to meet some unspoken expectations. When we paint the fence, I point out the places they've missed. When dinner's running late, I chide them for not setting the table and getting the drinks. I urge them to work, as if by being perfect, they can prove their love. Just as I could not save my father from his fears, my daughters cannot save me from the black muck inside that still says I'm not good enough. That even if I don't want to pick up a loaded gun and fire it, I must.

* * *

After Mr. William's death, I couldn't glimpse a gun case without wondering if Dad wanted to hurt himself too. Sometimes I'd stand beside the hot water tank and the gurgling sump pump that in spring rushed with water, threatened to overflow. The rifle cases leaned against the wall. I fingered my chest; touched the place where I believed the bullet entered Mr. William.

I begin to watch for signs of my own parents' sadness. And once I open my eyes to it, it seems impossible to ignore their disappointments. Dad hunches on the couch after work, newspaper dipping in his hands. At the dinner table he saws his food like it is made of cardboard. At bedtime, when my sister and I giggle and goof around, Dad unlaces his belt, stands in the frame of our door, demanding silence. The light from the kitchen behind his shadowed shape, his belt looped in one hand. "Goddamn you kids be quiet," he says. As he stands in the doorway it's like a rod has been jammed up my backside—I become immobile and still myself for the sound of the belt or his gruff return to the newspaper. I never know what will happen next.

I notice all the ways I force his mouth to twist, his shoulders to cast downward. My report card. Locking his keys in the car during an outing to my uncle's house. Spilling my milk at dinner and sometimes breakfast. Falling on my bike and coming into the house with bloodied knees. Each day I round up my failures until it becomes obvious that I am the cause of much of his displeasure. It is me.

I learned to follow him. I found that if I lingered around the car when he changed the oil or happened to be nearby when he figured out what he needed from the hardware store, he would invite me to join him. Together we went to the lumberyard with its sweet gummy new-wood smell or to the liquor store beneath the rows of fluorescent lights where we returned glass bottles of Coke for change. Burgers for groceries, Komo's for meat, the Chevy dealer on Torrence Avenue when he wanted to check out a new model.

I became the quiet accomplice to each errand. When the line at the hardware store was too long or they were out of the part he needed to fix the washer, he slammed his fist on the leg of his jeans, *goddamn it*, he said, eyes beady. I walked two steps to keep up with his one, but I was there. I took in his anger, ready to both bear witness and, later, absorb some of his fury.

# NOVEMBER 1, 1991

*Iowa City, Iowa*

When it happens, I am riding back to my dorm after volunteering to time at a men's swim meet. We're so smashed on the bus that I can only peer out the left side, so I don't see the flashing lights or feel the reverberation of the SWAT team. Unbeknownst to us, just a few feet away, men tumble out of an armed vehicle and surround Jessup Hall where Gang Lu has barricaded himself after taking his final shots. It's 4:03 p.m. and I brace myself for the weekend, the endlessness of it like a vacant lot.

*You've got to get out of your comfort zone*, my mother frequently advised, and I'd done it—agreed to help at the swim meet, only even standing around a swimming pool, something I had spent a good deal of my life doing, had felt off. I hadn't been sure which lane I was supposed to time and someone had to direct me at the last moment. I'd flushed red, embarrassed. I hadn't made any friends.

Later, eight of us crowd in Carol's dorm room and surround her TV as the newscasters repeat the same thing: "There has been a shooting on the campus of the University of Iowa. We will have more information shortly." The newscasters take turns repeating this until someone turns off the volume and passes around a bag of Doritos. Molly, our RA, appears at the door. Her thick face reminds me of the slabs of tenderloin that hang over the edge of the bun in the cafeteria. Molly wants to make sure everyone is all right. I sit on the floor and hold my knees, maybe rock them, some tiny bit of motion as information trickles in. The shooting started in Van Allen Hall, the very building where I'd attended Spanish that morning and ended not far from our dorm in Jessup Hall.

I look around the room at the other girls, many of whom on Thursday nights pack Carol's room to watch *90210*. We swoon over Luke Perry's hair and groan when Tori Spelling appears, all of us believing she is the worse actress of the lot; if our dads were directors, we'd be stars as well. After the show, a group of us sometimes goes out to the 19+ older bars—The Airliner, The Fieldhouse, even Vito's, if we are desperate, sipping Blue Hawaiians and Long Island Iced Teas, drinks like liquefied frosting, checking out the guys, waiting for them to approach. They never do, and so we return to our dorm where stale pizza boxes stack the hallways.

I try to find comfort in the presence of the other girls. I know their names. I know where they are from thanks to the paper cutouts Molly taped to our doors back in August. I don't say it, but I think: *What would keep the shooter from charging here to the second floor of Burge Hall and continuing his spree?*

Across the street, the Delts' volleyball pit stands vacant. No one's running down our floor, Red Hot Chili Peppers blaring. Phone lines are dead. Moments before going to Carol's room I'd picked up the receiver and heard nothing; it was like putting my ear against air. I've been in college for three months and feel the truth of it: I am alone.

We wait for the newscasters to return with an update, wait for the phones to start working, wait for our stomachs to grumble with hunger and the cafeteria to open when someone brings up the topic of guns.

Laura says guns should be illegal. Everyone nods in agreement; even me, although I do so mainly because it's what everyone expects. Liz, with her leather bomber jacket and wall of CDs. Amy with her plush comforter and eyelet shams. As a high schooler I borrowed a nautical-looking sweater from my grandma and paired it with a tan miniskirt, a look that rivaled the latest trend from The Limited, smiling and smiling and smiling no matter what was said. It's a face I've perfected. I've been practicing fitting in for years.

"It was one thing when people had to hunt for their dinner, but it isn't like that anymore," says Amy. "No one needs a gun."

I grab my knees tighter, think of my dad, the plastic milk jugs he set up in the backyard as targets. For years, I'd joined him out back as he'd load the pellet gun and arrange it in my arms, lifting an elbow, taking my chin and turning it. Telling me to line up the crosshairs and aim, the pellet plunking the jug side, water arcing the grass. *There's more to guns than killing people or animals*, I think. Most of the people I knew back home who owned guns, like Dad, had a deep reverence for them. Immediately after we shot the guns, Dad would carry them to the basement where he'd take them apart, spread the pieces out on the table where he'd sometimes set up a model train, then clean each part, pushing a wire brush through its segments, polishing it with a soft rag, then putting the gun away in its padded case.

"Why would anyone want to kill people?" asks Liz, as if such disdain isn't possible.

Sunday nights these same girls walk to the pedestrian mall for pizza at Rocky Roccoco's or grilled cheese sandwiches at Mickey's. When they ask me to join them, I say I'm not hungry, then wait a good ten minutes after my roommate leaves with them before I open a can of tuna, a sleeve of saltines. Afterward I take out the sheet of paper where I track expenses.

A little over a year ago, Mom and I toured campus on a hundred-degree day, humping over the hills that sloped from the Pentacrest, relishing the air-conditioned Union. Within minutes of stepping onto campus I felt a sort of déjà vu. I knew it was where I was supposed to spend the next four years of my life. That night, holding the stiff brochure, Dad said we couldn't afford it, and I burst into tears. "Hold on now, Carl," said Mom. "Let's just see." Soon after, Dad took a second job. Soon after, he said, "We might be able to do this."

Yet now that I am here, I cannot deny that I don't quite fit in. I try hard to say and do what is expected. One of the highlights is mail. Dad writes me once a week on plain paper with his distinctive blocky print. He'll tell me about mowing the lawn and how he attended my sister's volleyball game. He says Grandma came for dinner and made an apple pie. When he tells me to study hard and says Love Dad, I know he means it. Sometimes after reading his letter, I'll turn it over and trace the imprint of his pen, as if the touch might reinforce my own existence.

I don't remember what they serve that night in the cafeteria. I don't remember the clothes that I wore or who I sat with at dinner. But I remember the empty feeling that pitted my belly, like the first hours of the flu.

That night I can't sleep. I retrace the morning's steps to and from Van Allen Hall. I see the double doors to the side entrance of Dubuque Avenue, from which I now knew Gang Lu had left after shooting four faculty and a graduate student in the space physics program. I see the waxed floors, the stairwell I take to get to the basement classroom and the musical voice of my professor. *¿Qué te gusta hacer? ¿Que música te gusta?*

I see the heavily painted cinderblock walls, that windowless space. I see the herd of desks, someone rushing into our classroom with a gun. It could have been me or my roommate or any of us. I think of those who were shot dead and their loved ones, and tears leak into my hairline. The sadness I feel expands as I think of my own family, offering me affection I may never be able to show myself. An immenseness swells beneath the raft of my loneliness. As I set sail, the uncertainty moves in—great storm clouds that blanket the horizon.

NOVEMBER 2, 1991
*Iowa City, Iowa*

Copies of *The Daily Iowan* stretch the dorm hallway like flattened dominoes. Before I change out of my pajamas, I grab a copy and sit outside our room while my roommate sleeps. A photo of Gang Lu absorbs the front page. He wears an olive-green T-shirt and heavy black glasses. Alongside his picture are the headshots and names of the deceased.

I look closely at their faces. Try to determine whether we've crossed paths. I read the timeline of events—all of it took twelve minutes. Figured that after Gang Lu had mowed down T. Anne Cleary and the student temp Miya Sioson, he barricaded himself inside an empty classroom, taken off the jacket worn throughout the rampage, and shot himself, I had been standing on the pool deck on the other side of campus as the swimmers tore through the water and I clocked their progress.

I read the article again and again. Learn that Gang Lu had been planning his attack and suicide for months after a fellow graduate student received the dissertation award Lu believed he deserved. Later, in the letter they discover in his jacket pocket, he wrote: "Since then I have sworn myself that I would revenge at any cost, sooner or later."

I imagine his fury as a deep black hole. Nothing I read helps me better understand the shooter, his anguish. I keep seeing the stairwell to my classroom in Van Allen Hall, the green stretch of the Pentacrest.

The ringing phone perforates the morning's silence. I dart into the room, grab the receiver, and pull the phone's cord with me into the hall. It's Mom.

"Melissa? Thank God," she says. "We tried to call you last night."

"All the lines were down," I tell her.

"I know," she says. Her voice a hug. Relief swings through me followed by a swift and sudden surge of homesickness. "We knew you were okay because your letter said you'd be timing at the swim meet. Thank God almighty. Are you okay?"

I tell her that I am.

"Dad wants to say something."

In the pause I see our kitchen table, Dad's mug of Lipton tea with the half-submerged slice of lemon. The plate he used for his two slices of toast now spotted with crumbs.

"Are you okay?" he asks, his voice sleep ridged.

I nod, and then say that I am. "My roommate's still asleep. I'm in the hall."

"Was it bad?" he asks.

"We hung out in someone's dorm room most of the night. No one went out or anything. It was scary." I can't tell him or Mom what I've been thinking about all night—what had woken me up well before my roommate: If something happened to me, I didn't know if I'd be missed.

"When they bombed the math building at Wisconsin, I was this poor grad student with a wife and young baby. I just wanted to graduate." It was 1970 and Dad has shared the story previously, only this time I listen closer as he describes the early morning phone call he received from a fellow pharmacy student before he headed into the lab. Later, standing alongside the pharmacy building that faced Sterling Hall, the stench of ammonia nitrate stung his eyes. Smoke billowed up from the crater where part of the building once stood. "They killed a graduate student who had been pulling an all-nighter, just like I'd done countless times. The guy had three kids. Can you imagine? Those three kids would grow up without a father." It was something Dad, who had lost his own father when he was fourteen years old, had been unable to put away. Years later, when I am stuck in a dead-end teaching job, dealing with a priggish colleague who leaves threatening notes in my mailbox, I'll be unable to eat or sleep and when I let myself think maybe it's too much, I'll take comfort in knowing I am single and do not have kids.

He's told me bits and pieces about the bombing. Now, for the first time, I picture him—just a few years older than me with sideburns and thick glasses, a newborn baby and the sudden shock of destruction. "That must have been hard," I say.

"It was terrible. I just wanted to get out of there. I just wanted to graduate."

Dorm doors begin to open as people leave their rooms with rumpled hair, pillow-etched faces.

"Please. Please be careful," Dad says. I promise him I will.

\* \* \*

Later that morning after pancakes that taste like they've been mixed with dust, I unlock my ten-speed from the rack out front and ride the cobblestone streets past the president's mansion, the Tri Delts house, and Mercy Hospital. The sky's the color of drying glue and I ride without destination, wind on my face.

I've been biking no more than fifteen minutes when I happen upon a cemetery surrounded by a stone wall. I've seen it before but now I stop, lean my bike on its side and step through an opening in the stones. I follow a gravel path. Large craggy trees line the way, their branches crisscross overhead. Brittle knots of leaves roll alongside my step.

The weight of the past day catches up with me. Each step immense. My body heavy with exhaustion. Back in my closet at home I keep a box of remembrances—a crumpled Kleenex from my grandpa's funeral, my first bra, the yearbook from eighth grade, ribbons from swim meets. I had imagined myself continuing to add items and at eighty-something going through the box and understanding my life's purpose. The idea of being the same person, of bringing this loneliness with me nearly paralyzes my eighteen-year-old self. So many days I had returned from high school, finished a glass of orange juice and slid beneath the blankets of my bed, grateful for the annihilation of sleep, how hours later, in the sullen darkness, I'd be disappointed to wake. Here, away from my dorm, there's no denying it: The despair I'd left in high school, inside my parents' house, is still with me.

In this Iowan fall, the air smells of decay and wood smoke. The gravel beneath the soles of my tennis shoes reminds me of each step. I imagine lying down in the cool quiet of the cemetery. There were days I had wanted nothing more than such stillness. Instead, I look out at the rows of headstones, the grass sloping slightly in front of some of them. When the breeze reaches for me, I lift my face, try to cup it with both hands.

# THE ELEMENTS OF FICTION

*To build a successful story, many writers employ a structure of conflict-crisis-resolution.*

*Start with conflict right away so that the reader is plunged into the problem of your narrative. A memorable beginning often includes shards of the conflict.*

I learned in my English education classes to honor my students' reactions to a story, so the first time Devers interrupts me in class during a discussion of Joyce Carol Oates's "Where Are You Going, Where Have You Been?" with "If Connie is going to dress and act like that, she's got things coming to her," I pause. Look at the other students.

"Okay, so you think Connie is in some way responsible for the violence that is alluded to at the end of the story," I say. "Anyone else? What do others think about Connie?" My question hangs unanswered. The lack of response stings. I'm twenty-seven years old and teaching college-level composition and creative writing for the first time in a small town in Utah. This is a one-year position, but I'm hopeful it will develop into something long term, something I'll be able to hold up to my dad and say, *See? I did it.*

I've spent all summer crafting a course syllabus that will not just inform students about the elements of fiction, but also expose them to some of the finest examples of the short story form. This is a class I would have loved to have taken as an undergraduate and now I am teaching it.

Later that night as I prepare for our next class, the story titles take me far from my kitchen table. Suddenly I am eight or nine, waiting on our front porch for my dad to return from work to take me to the library for our weekly trip.

Then I am a high school student tucked in bed, struggling in algebra, yet staying up all night to read *Catcher in the Rye* while the rest of my family sleeps.

Later I am twenty-five and stuffing boxes into my Chevy, getting ready to leave for graduate school. After years of taking night classes while teaching junior high English, studying for the GRE and applying to numerous graduate schools, I've finally gained admittance. All of this has been made more challenging by my family. My dad in particular thinks an MFA doesn't make much sense. There are no specific jobs that warrant a degree in creative writing. He worries I won't be able to support myself.

"Are you sure you want to leave your teaching job?" my mom asks. "They've been so good to you."

"It's not real. Fiction isn't real," my dad says as I carry bins of clothes from my parents' basement to the backseat of my car. "What you're doing isn't real." I slam the door. Tell him I have more packing to do. Meanwhile, his words rattle me, settle deep inside.

I wish I could tell him what it's like to draft a story, how I lose track of time and the ideas in my head unspool and as much as I am the one writing the story, I am also listening to it and what it wants to become. But I can't tell him this and expect him to understand, so I don't say anything. When he later learns I've been offered a position teaching creative writing to college students, he tells me about the

English class he took in high school and how that teacher connected the stories from their anthology to actual historical events. "The class was just unbelievable," he says.

I nod, say "That must have been great." Then I think: *I want to be that sort of teacher*—someone whose class is so memorable that when a student talks about it with their adult kids, their voices radiate admiration.

## SETTING

*Where your story takes place can be just as important as the story itself. Ask yourself, why must this story occur here?*

That weekend I fill a water bottle, lace my hiking boots, and drive to Cedar Mountain. I hike along the dry riverbed of Coal Creek. Cacti spike through the sand of the crusted earth. I focus on the day, its blue brightness and how the sun settles on my shoulders like a warm and patient hand. Pausing at an overlook, I take in the miniaturized houses below me. I hadn't realized I'd been moving so quickly. A posted sign warns of mountain lions, which follow packs of deer during the winter. A high degree of risk can ruin any enjoyment. I know this firsthand. After applying to over thirty teaching jobs, this was my only offer. I've moved to Utah from Chicago. My boyfriend, Pete, lives in Ohio. I eat pasta in front of the TV, squirrel away time to write on Thursdays and Saturdays. Sometimes boys in white short-sleeved shirts and dark pants knock on my apartment door. Missionaries. They ask if I believe in God or a higher power. I smile and say I have somewhere I need to be, thank them, and close the door. I am a lapsed Catholic, but refrain from sharing this.

I have not received word of a publication in months and find myself looking for signs to confirm my lack of success—a form rejection from a publication that last year sent a full letter, a good friend whose work I've always considered on par with my own receives his first book deal. A book is the surest way to contract renewal and eventually a tenure-track job. Once I have that sort of job, I'll receive more money and better benefits and job security. I'll be legitimate. So, as I grade, or plan class activities and assignments, I think about student evaluations. And anytime I think about students, Devers worms his way into my thoughts.

When I am caught up with grading, I drive an hour to a larger town and park at a plaza with a used bookstore. After filling a bag with books, I buy myself secondhand clothes to wear teaching—polyester blouses and a lemon-colored sweater with zig-zagged stitching. Away from my desk and books, I linger in the parked car with my purchases watching families at a nearby ice cream shop gesture with their paper cups and tiny spoons. Laughter falls from their packed mouths as the desert sun spreads an orange-sherbet hue across the sky.

## CHARACTERS

*The goal for your characters is to make the reader believe they are living, breathing beings. We learn about characters from their appearance, what they say, their actions, their thoughts, and what the narrator tells us.*

When I lecture on the direct and indirect methods of characterization, jotting notes on the board, passing out a recent article from *The Writer's Chronicle*, Devers is quiet. He wears a bandanna tied over his shaved head and his biceps, which usually hulk out the armholes of his tank tops, seem smaller, contained. On those days the students seem more engaged. "When you write, you can vary the approach to a character so the narrative closely identifies with a protagonist or has a greater separation from them. It's known as psychic distance." I grow giddy as my students jot notes, transpose my words and ideas onto paper.

We continue with our discussion and I welcome the back-and-forth, how their thoughts open to new ways of thinking.

The first short exercise I assign in fiction writing is character development. One pregnant girl writes about a quilter. Another student writes of a character watching his love interest hang from the side of a cliff, rocks tumbling past her shoulders. Devers writes about a woman washing windows in a short dress, her nipples poking through the sheer fabric while her husband thinks about shooting her in the head—one pop, two.

I tell myself that the bloodshed in his exercise is the result of television and bad movies, then make a note encouraging him to use more details and interiority to move the scene. Secretly I feel a trickle of dread. Why had he drawn his protagonist like a prostitute? Did he consider how the other females in the class, or I might feel? In fiction writing, students had free range to write whatever compelled them—within reason. My being here should make this obvious.

## DIALOGUE

*Through dialogue, the actual words characters speak unfold before us directly. Dialogue can provide further access to your character's inner life.*

Two days later, Devers stands in the open door of my office with his returned writing exercise and a yellow highlighter, his mouth firm. I smile and offer him a seat, ask how I can be of help.

Without responding, he pulls the chair as close as he can, his breath grazing my bare shoulder. He turns to the second page of his story, opens the marker, and highlights four sentences, then snaps the cap onto the marker and slams it on my desk before pushing the paper toward me. "What's that?" he asks, poking the page at one of my handwritten comments. I haven't finished reading the sentences when he says, "Description. You said there wasn't enough."

"We can always use more. I want to be able to *see* his distaste for his wife."

He flips a few more pages and highlights another section. This time he points to the paragraph, pounding his fist on my desk. Two pens roll off the desk and plink onto the floor. "Right there," he snaps. "Description."

I choose not to pick up the pens. My shoulders and neck and back have gone stiff, as if in one moment I've been hollowed out and filled with molten steel that's already set. I think slowly, measure my words. Everything necessitates exactness.

"Yes," I say. "You have some great ideas, now I'd just like to see you expand these further."

I repeat this phrase three times.

He highlights more sections. "Are you even old enough to teach this class? I hope you've at least been to college."

"I have a master's," I chirp and my head jerks at this. I'd been hired to teach fiction writing. I'd already published a handful of stories and won an award that sent me to a writing workshop at Francis Ford Coppola's Belize estate. Yet none of this matters. There is only the cheap laminate desk where Devers has set his story, the weak overhead light, my thin voice.

"Well, you don't look old enough to teach this class." My mouth fills with sand. Somehow, I swallow. "I'm old enough. Trust me." But even I don't believe what I say.

He slams his chair back. Leaves. I clench and unclench my hands, breathing hard until it comes to me. Devers knows the truth: I shouldn't be here.

TENSION

*Manipulate tension in your piece by letting characters encounter obstacles that keep them from getting what they want. To ramp up tension's pulse, combine this with danger and risks.*

I discover the hours for lap swim at the campus pool, a new facility of eight lanes, and a diving well surrounded on two sides by walls of glass. As I swim, I think about my classes. With every lap, my head clears. My composition students are mostly freshmen and they seem resigned to my lectures, our essay assignments. But when I think about fiction writing, I don't know where to go. I already feel as if I've failed. My interactions with Devers have caused me to arrive at class edgy and uncertain. I seldom smile. I prepare extra notes and look at these during class, anything to steady my nerves. I decide this is the best way to proceed. To focus on lectures and keep discussion at a minimum. To just get through the semester.

I'm explaining to our class the advantages and disadvantages of the first-person point of view in creating tension when Devers interrupts me saying, "It's also easier to use when you're writing description."

The other students watch me. "Actually, the third person is more suited for description," I say. Devers writes something in his notebook and remains subdued the rest of class. A small win.

I put the students into small groups and hide behind the low chatter as they discuss Gabriel García Márquez's "A Very Old Man with Enormous Wings." It opens when Pelayo, after heavy rains, discovers an old man with large wings lying face down in the mud of their yard. He and the townspeople take turns trying to determine who the old man is. When the winged man ultimately leaves, Pelayo's wife is relieved "because he is no longer an annoyance in her life." We are approaching midterms and each time I am in class, I feel the same hope that Devers might one day disappear and then I could teach the way I hoped.

Devers interrupts two more times before class ends and I am grateful when the students gather their belongings and leave.

Two communication majors—Camden and Julie—who usually sit near me explain that Devers acts similarly in all his classes. "It's nothing personal," Camden says. Both he and Julie hope to become broadcast journalists and talk excitedly about life after graduation.

"I can't wait to get out of here," says Julie. It's true—this small Utah town is unlike any place I've ever lived. The only pizzeria closes at eight o'clock and serves a crust that reminds me of stale bread, but the tamales at Lupita's are divine, smothered in a peppery red sauce and served with a side of mashed avocado.

Violet, a professor of French, who is a transplant from Milwaukee, invites me on a hike one Saturday morning in another small dusty town where afterward we sip iced coffee on an outdoor patio. If we sit long enough, I'm certain I'll see tumbleweeds blow past.

We talk about movies and books, our parents and siblings. I feel myself relaxing and think we will be friends. Violet seems fun and easygoing. I could learn from her. I tell her about Devers and she nods for a long time before speaking. "You just need to ignore him. Act like he doesn't even exist."

STAKES

*What your character wants must matter and the reader must sense this desire.*

It's late October. We are more than halfway through the semester. In the dwindling minutes of class when I am explaining our story assignment, Devers says, "I can make her blush. Hey, did you see that? She's blushing again." I reach up and press a hand against my cheek. Everything feels hot. I talk but I'm sure my words wobble. At the most vital intersections of my life, I have chosen passivity. I've tapped down my opinions and wants, pushed them off to the side. This will be an exception. I email Devers that afternoon and tell him that I need to speak with him before our next class. My anger threads with fear, and then I am pissed all over again. I've moved halfway across the country to teach. That's why I went to school. That's why I'm here.

The following day, he knocks on my office door and I gesture to a seat, tell him to leave the door open.

"I'm going to explain why I've asked you here. To start with, I don't appreciate being interrupted in class." I sit tall and do not take my eyes off his. A furious river charges my veins.

Devers straightens. "I didn't realize I'd offended you." He pauses. "I like to talk with you," he says, and he seems genuinely surprised. I momentarily soften. "Since I'm paying tuition, I try to have close relationships with each of my professors."

Something about the implication that he pays my salary sends me spinning. I hold my gaze and feel myself gathering strength like a cyclone that builds force with every bend. "The university encourages *respectful* relationships between teachers and students."

"I come in and talk to all my other teachers. I'm trying to get the most out of my education."

"Talking is encouraged. Arguing or interrupting is not. And comments about my age or the fact you can make me blush are inappropriate." His face is pulled tight, like a baby who is about to wail, but has yet to suck in a mouthful of air. I ask if he has any questions.

"No," he mutters.

"Then I expect your behavior to change." With these words, everything beneath my skin shudders. I want to simultaneously tear off his head and throw a fist into the air for speaking up and keeping my cool. Instead, we stare at each other for an extended moment, and then he picks up his backpack and swings it onto his shoulder, concealing his tattoo, the face of a lion. He leaves in a huff and for the rest of the day I feel jubilant. I should have stood up for myself weeks ago.

Later I don't feel so sure. I had taken note of Devers's age, the tattoo, and expected his distrust. What did I really know about him?

Didn't I discourage students from crafting one-sided characters? Even unlikeable characters could be redeeming.

I had so wanted to be seen as a writer worthy of teaching college students that I had let Devers define me—maybe welcomed it. Then, doubting myself, I'd invited his critique. No symposium or class had prepared me to teach a student like Devers. The fault was partially mine.

CRISIS

*The last conflict in your piece is the crisis. This is when everything for your protagonist is at its worst. The crisis usually occurs close to the story's end.*

The following class, Devers wears sunglasses throughout the fifty minutes and props his feet on an empty desk. Every few minutes he punches the seat with the heels of his high tops and pulls the desk forward so the legs of the desk screech. He turns to the side so he faces the hallway, arms crossed over his chest. During a discussion of James Baldwin's "Sonny's Blues," Devers tears sheets of paper from his notebook, rolls them into balls, and tosses them on the floor at the exact moment I speak. I stop counting after the fourth sheet. His profile is grim. Should I call him out in front of everyone? The other students seem to be ignoring me; I don't blame them and on some level this contempt seems appropriate. I'm the one who is supposed to be in charge.

The dreams begin when I learn from a colleague that Devers was recently released from prison. In my dreams, he pushes me down and grabs my arms, holds them high over my head. He brandishes a knife and it gleams in the fat of his palm. This part of the dream occurs when I am in the process of taking off my clothes. Oftentimes, he is the one removing them.

I always wake screaming.

I check and double-check the deadbolt lock on my apartment door. I peer in the closets and pull back the shower curtain, looking for signs of him. At my request the landlord installs a security bar along the sliding glass doors, although it will not stop Devers. He will smash his fist through the glass and pay no heed to pain.

I sit down to write, but no stories hold my interest. My mind returns to the fiction writing class. I berate myself for my obvious lack of authority and inability to control Devers. If I were stricter, if I lectured more, and asked fewer open-ended questions I might wield more power. If I published a book, I'd feel surer of my place standing at the front of class. If my family hadn't stared at me blankly when I told them I wanted to be a writer there might be less to prove.

One weekend I visit Pete thousands of miles from Utah, and I wake yelling. "Who are you? Which one are you?"

"Shh," Pete tells me, "It's me. I'm right here."

I hear the scorched sound of my black velvet dress from high school, feel my body moored beneath my date as an undergraduate.

"You're okay," Pete says. *Not yet*, I think.

## THEME

*Theme is what your story is ultimately about. All the details of a piece contribute to the story's overall theme and beliefs.*

Four weeks remain in the semester. Devers's story is nineteen pages long. In it a man chops a woman into pieces and drops her into a rusted footlocker. Another man finds her, attracted by the stench of her rotting body, and puts her back together—miraculously, she returns to life. He proceeds to fuck her the way she's always desired—they screw for two days straight and "she'd never been happier."

I read it until the eighth page and then the web of knots in my stomach forces me to push it aside. How many times can a woman be raped and stabbed and plead for more? It's me in his story. It's every woman.

Later I'll find out he's been forcing this story into the hands of writing lab assistants—female ones—asking them to read it out loud, to help him with his grammar, he'll say. When a page later it says that the woman's head is bashed into the wall, I imagine myself as that woman and put the story aside.

I think of those tutors, eighteen, nineteen years old, reading his piece because he has asked them to do so. That's it. This isn't about me. It's the fact that I'm female.

I am reminded of the scene from *Revenge of the Nerds* when nerdy Lewis Skolnick, who has fallen in love with Betty Childs, steals her boyfriend's Darth Vader costume and follows her into the fun house. When Lewis's fingers tentacle her breasts, I waited for her to realize those aren't her boyfriend's hands or body or smell or touch. When Betty tries to pry off the mask, Lewis holds it firm and the two end up doing it in a bounce house. The movie is supposed to be funny, only I never laughed at that part. When Lewis reveals who he really is, I waited for Betty to deck him or throw him off her. Instead, Betty says, "God, you were wonderful."

Any fear she had melts into attraction. In the film, deception became a turn-on. What would make someone think reality was any different?

This is how I imagine it will unfold: he'll creep into my garage late one night. He'll wait over three hours and at some point, nearly give up; returning to his van parked one block north. He has an exam in his Renaissance class the following day—no point in doing poorly in two classes this semester. But something draws him back to the bitch's garage to look one last time. When he sees the blue glimmer of her Subaru turn the corner, his mouth breaks into a grin. She has come home to him.

Moments later, he's standing outside the open garage, waiting for her to turn off the ignition. The car door opens, slams shut. The garage door begins its slow descent. She turns, takes four steps around to the back of the car—bitch doesn't have a clue—and then he scurries under the closing garage door. She turns, her lips just beginning to separate when he claps his hand over her mouth.

RESOLUTION

*Every story must demonstrate that the crisis has been resolved. Readers want to see that the protagonist has changed. The best resolutions are implied and resonate beyond the story's end.*

After talking with my chair and filing a complaint, the response is quick and informal. The head of the Sexual Harassment Committee will arrange the meeting. During introductions she will mistakenly call him by his full name. "It's Devers," he corrects her. "And I want a lawyer."

"That won't be necessary, Devers. We just want to hear your side of the story, so this hearing doesn't become more formal."

"I know my rights and I know when I'm being ganged up on."

I've worn the TJ Maxx suit from my job interview: ivory with a light-brown plaid. I try and drum up the fury I'd felt when I learned Devers had been forcing his work on writing tutor staff, but my energy is nonexistent. We sit around an oval table, Devers off to one side. The air feels harshly antiseptic as if any moment someone could announce visiting hours will soon end.

The head of security reminds him that his parole officer will be invited to a formal inquiry. In the silence, I proceed.

Reading from a typed copy I tell the committee about his comments in class, read notes from our conference, and last, I'll read excerpts from his recent story. I don't trust the words to come from my mouth on their own.

He interrupts. "I didn't mean to offend her. I wasn't trying to. I respect her."

I am only a pronoun.

The committee asks what I propose and for the first time in months, I speak freely.

"You cannot interrupt me in class or make comments about my age. No matter how old I am, I've been hired to teach fiction writing. That's why I'm here." My hands shake. I know what I want to say. It comes to me clear and clean like when I get to the end of the story and it nearly writes itself. "I don't feel like I can accurately assess Devers's work this semester."

I glare at the bones of Devers's skull. "I don't want Devers in my class nor do I ever want him in my classes." The committee supports my recommendation and Devers will finish the semester in independent study with a male colleague. The head of security reminds Devers he has no reason to lurk around the English department or my office. Later that day, this same security officer will supply me with information about Devers's van, a green Plymouth Voyager with Missouri plates. He'll also hand me his business card, tell me to call for any reason. "I don't even know why Devers is here. But I promise his probation officer will be interested in hearing about all this." We shake hands.

After he leaves, I keep thinking about it. Why *is* Devers in my class? To remind me of how much I have yet to learn? That just because I teach doesn't mean I'm successful at it? Maybe in the end, the ability to write a story is just as important as understanding when to put one aside.

For the rest of the day, I won't be able to shake the image of Devers sitting alone at the table. There was so much about him that I would never know. He had wanted to write fiction and I had wanted to teach. I longed to be a competent professional, more than just someone with boobs, an easy target for her husband's fury or the punchline for a gag. My fears had gotten in the way of all of it.

If this time in my life were a work of fiction, perhaps I would poke a finger into Devers's chest and call him a liar or tell him in front of class that his stories need a good deal of work and he was far from knowing it all.

I can tell you some things about student writers. They are shy about their work, hesitant to share story drafts. They clear their throats and straighten themselves in their seats before reading their writing aloud. Dialogue can be scattershot or overly explained. Sometimes every bit of speech includes a tag: *he or she or they said* as if there is no way the reader will figure out this is a conversation and what these people say and do reveals character. Yet I've also seen how a student's face gleams when other students respond to their stories. The biggest compliment they offer is when they ask one another, *Did that really happen to you?*

*Nah*, the student will say, grinning. *I made it up.* They do not understand their power. But I can coax those ideas forward, to see the half-raised hand and call each student by name.

# PEACH PIT

If owning a dog is preparation for having kids, Pete and I are failing, I think, as we sit on folding chairs at the emergency vet clinic with Cooper, our three-year-old lab-shepherd mix. We brought him here after he swallowed a peach pit. At the front desk, they explained how the cost for our visit will be determined by the severity of Cooper's illness. In his case, he's breathing fine, but the peach pit is likely still making its way through his intestines. Time will tell. Meanwhile, we sit and watch and wait. Outside, the snort and suck of traffic pays little respect to the hushed state of the waiting room.

Up to this point, I've been able to refrain from asking Pete, *what were you thinking?* But as the bulldog to our left oozes into a bloody bath towel that's been wrapped around his head and his owner wipes tears from her eyes, without prompting, Pete speaks up.

"I didn't know he was going to swallow it."

"He's a dog! You gave him a peach!"

"I only wanted him to take a bite," he said. "It was such an amazing peach."

I fold my arms, cross my legs, and choose to stare at another ailing animal. We've already been here an hour during which time we've seen several other pets arrive bloodied, stinking of vomit, some so still in stature that I wonder if they are even breathing. While each has been taken away for treatment behind a door labeled No Admittance, we have yet to see any of these animals return to the waiting room wagging their tails or pawing at the icily conditioned air. Really, this urgent care center is the last place we can afford to be. We bought our first house late last year, Pete's making the minimum payment on his school loans, and our cars are old. Cooper has allergies, so we special order hypoallergenic food from the vet. Sometimes he takes antihistamines as well. I hide these pills in dollops of liver sausage and let him lick my fingers afterward.

We live in Evergreen Park, a blue-collar town a few miles southwest of Chicago. It has a strong Irish Catholic population. Sturdy brick bungalows and robust flower boxes are pierced with decorative flags that say Bee Happy with an image of a bumblebee.

So far we've pulled out the kitchen cabinets, ripped off the wallpaper, used heat guns and mini spatulas to loosen the plastic tiles from the kitchen and bathrooms, the discarding pieces falling at our feet like shingles. While wearing thick work gloves, we removed decades-old blue carpeting from the stairs and living room, and then crawling, applied crowbars to yank thick toothed staples, stopping only to swig water from the same plastic tumbler or eat a handful of pretzels. Both our parents had expressed displeasure when they first toured the house, a 1942 Georgian, but with its original french windows and mahogany trim, we pointed out that the house had good bones. In fact, within taking three steps into the foyer, I told Pete, *This is it!* This was the house for us. Such a proclamation only happened to me on a few occasions—when I spied my first bike, a Huffy Strawberry Sizzler, at Kmart, and the first time Pete asked me to dance at a mutual friend's wedding in California. We were twenty-seven years old and when I look at Pete quickly, I see him again as if for the first time.

He'd been spending the week running throughout the state of California. Pete kept a jar of Skippy and a loaf of bread in his rental car, a jug of water. Each day he'd drive to a state park, put on his running shoes, coat himself in sunscreen, and run fifteen or twenty miles through the redwoods and on trails that followed the Pacific coast.

I remember thinking two things the first time I met Pete. One: I thought he was the groom's brother. Two: I thought he was skinny. But it wasn't until I'd enjoyed three gin and tonics, when I put my hands on Pete's shoulders during a slow dance that I felt a jolt of electricity. I looked at him—really looked at him for the first time. What was that?

The next day I flew back to Chicago. I was living with my parents that summer, preparing to move to Pennsylvania where I'd accepted a position teaching creative writing at a state college while finishing my first story collection. Then that week, a letter arrived. It was from Pete—the guy from the wedding—and as I unfolded it and read it for the first time, I recalled that charge from the dance floor. I peered at the return address, the handwriting nearly illegible, then penned him a response. The letters went back and forth between our residences for months. We wrote about our days, the books we were reading, music we adored. In those letters I could be myself in a way I could not in real life.

Pete says he simply thought I was funny and good looking and that he wanted to keep talking with me, which is why he switched places with a friend so he could sit beside me at the reception. Some people call this a firefly friendship or an instant connection. Pete says he felt this immediate bond at the Humane Society when he met Cooper.

Soon after signing the paperwork for our mortgage, we began to talk about getting a dog. These were spirited discussions over coffee and the Sunday *New York Times* as we sat in our backyard beneath a honey locust, one of the oldest trees in the neighborhood. It stood directly behind the house, with its craggy bark and mossy patches, leaves as fine as antique lace. "This yard is calling for a dog. Don't you want a dog?" Pete asked, leaning over to rub the side of his face on my forehead or pretending to hump my leg.

"You're a nut," I said, and pushed him away.

I did want a dog, but there was no rush. The dog we had growing up—J.R.—was a mutt that had aggressive tendencies. We couldn't take him to be groomed and could barely run a brush down his back without him snapping. Mom blamed his aggression on the fact that they'd never gotten him fixed. One fall day after raking, my brother fell back into a pile of leaves and J.R. jumped onto him and bit his face, leaving a parcel of skin hanging from his lip that later had to be cauterized by a plastic surgeon. Dogs were unpredictable. And yet I could also recall cuddling near J.R. as he slept on the green scrap of carpet we kept in the corner of the kitchen. How I could pet his back end and he seldom growled. Sometimes, when I was fighting with my sister, I would talk to J.R. and tell him my problems. But it had been years since I'd used a dog as a confessional. Pete's quiet strength steered me through personal and professional crises during the past four years of marriage, and we were in a good place. Renovations were moving along and we'd talked about planting another tree in the backyard, maybe making space along the fence for a garden.

Unbeknownst to me, soon after we signed the mortgage, Pete had begun to visit the Humane Society and one afternoon, while walking through the howling, barking cacophony of cages, he spotted Cooper. Poop streaked his backside but his eyes were bright, his tail and bottom wiggling nonstop behind the grate. Pete told me later he couldn't wait to meet him up close.

I could have been offended by his decision to shop for a dog without me, but I was too swept up in Pete's excitement. Pete frequently wore blue T-shirts, but now the color set off his eyes further, infused them with light. There didn't seem much harm in checking out the dogs, letting Pete's delight burn a little longer.

Two days later I agreed to go to the Humane Society.

They led us to a small glassed-in reception area where prospective pet owners could get to know an animal. There was a small wooden bench along the wall and a few wayward toys. During our twenty-minute meet-and-greet, Cooper's tail never stopped wagging. He looked intently at Pete and kept bringing him toys—a rubber ball, a soggy stuffed duck, while I sat there and watched the two of them in what seemed like the reunion of old friends. "Isn't he the best?"

The dog was cute and energetic, but he paid me little attention. My feelings were lukewarm at best. Pete meanwhile crouched down and used a knot of rope so he and Cooper could play tug. As I watched them, a cool trickle of jealousy unspooled inside me. Someday we planned to have a family. What if our kids preferred Pete to me? They'd likely grow up seeing me as the fuddy-duddy, telling them not to wear their good clothes out to play and to take off their shoes at the door. Meanwhile Pete would be following them outside, rolling around on the ground and getting dirty.

I didn't know that I was ready to be the unpopular one. But Pete was resolute, blinking at me from where he crouched with Cooper. "This is a gem of a dog."

Later, after we'd paid the fees for his shots and led him to the backseat of Pete's car, I sat beside Cooper and smiled. Well, we were doing it. We had a dog. I straightened my shoulders and patted Cooper on the head for longer than I needed to. It was time for him to begin liking me. I beamed. "We are taking you home!" I announced, and fastened my seatbelt. I rolled down the window and Cooper stuck out his head, panting in the wind. At one point he turned back to look at me. I was about to touch him when he lowered his chin and vomited half-digested kibble all over my shorts. I screamed.

"It's okay, hang in there," said Pete as he jerked the wheel to the right and pulled into a Red Lobster parking lot. He opened the door where I sat with my back pressed against the seat, Cooper's muck coating my bare legs. "Oh no, buddy. You have an upset stomach?" he scratched Cooper behind the ears and cooed that we'd be home soon.

I understood the dog was sick, but he wasn't the only uncomfortable one. "Pete, what about me?" I gestured at my legs and feet.

He told me to hold tight and scrounged around the trunk for an old towel.

After drying myself as best I could, we switched places. Pete took my seat in the back of the car and Cooper placed his head in Pete's lap, then promptly fell asleep.

* * *

A bell rings and the entrance to the clinic opens. A couple carries in what looks to be a cat nestled deep inside a sleeping bag. Across the room, a dog makes a low lopsided growl but wiggles its tail as if it is no longer sure what is a threat.

Outside the streetlights have flipped on and traffic softened. Rush hour is over. "Maybe he'll just pass it," Pete says. Cooper looks up at us. For the past three hours he's divided his body underneath the seats of our chairs, head on paws. All the reading we did on the internet before coming to the clinic said a fruit pit could obstruct a dog's bowels, which would require emergency surgery. "I don't know," I say. "What if something happens? What if he gets sick?" I wasn't thinking about how the money we had planned to use to replace the cloth wiring was now probably going to the emergency vet clinic.

"Then we'll come back," Pete says. "At least now we know how to get here."

I tell myself he's right. There's more than one way to care for a dog. Maybe I could get dirty right alongside Pete. He would show me the way.

We stand from our folding chairs and a few pet owners look up at us, surprised by such sudden actions in the hallowed waiting room. Cooper could still stop breathing or worse and we'd be home alone with him, unsure what to do. "We'll figure it out," Pete says, and I believe him, follow him out the door, back home, where eventually middle-of-the-night feedings and fevers await us, and we take our chances together, as a family.

# THE FACTS OF LIFE

My first pregnancy started with a digital thermometer. When my alarm went off in the morning, I stuck the thermometer beneath my tongue and remained still, waited for it to beep. I jotted the temperature on a pad of paper at my bedside. Twelve days after my last period, my temperature dipped—the textbook symptom of an egg's impending release. We tried that night, two nights later and the evening after that, and on the last night, when I imagined the egg in the process of descending, making its way down the fallopian tubes, I held my knees to my chest like they do in the movies. I was thirty-four years old and at this point, I was simply hoping to have a healthy child. Pete asked me what I was doing.

"I'm helping your guys with a little gravity."

"My guys? They love swimming."

I laughed at the absurdity of this. When we went to the pool, Pete could barely float.

We settled into one another. Pete put his arm around me, and I imagined his swimmers making their way in one great wave, tails flickering, heads steely and intent. I breathed in his spicy deodorant, behind that, the sweet tang of sweat. Beside him, everything calmed. The transformation from one cell into two had begun.

\* \* \*

I learned about sex in fifth grade. Only they didn't call it that. It was a course titled Growth and Development and, before class began, each of us took home a photocopied consent form for our parents to sign.

Mrs. Jansen divided our class into boys and girls. In one week's time, five successive days after lunch, I knew the textbook purposes of fallopian tubes, vas deferens, sperm, egg, blastocyte, embryo, and menstruation. The sex act itself remained foggy.

I imagined my own parents sitting beside one another in bed, deciding to make me. They already had a little boy, so why not try for a girl?

In my mind, I saw them slip inside the powder room with its bare toilet and blue ruffled curtains, hips turned to the side so they could both fit in the tiny room. They faced one another. The light above the sink flickered. There was a new bar of Ivory in the soap dish, a box of Kleenex on the tank behind the toilet. A mirror hung from its plastic handle on the wall. They weren't wearing clothes, but their individual body parts remained unclear, blurred. "Let's make Melissa," they said in unison, and then smashed their bodies together, minds twined around the idea of creating a daughter.

By the time Dad clicked off the light and they slid beneath the covers, my life inside Mom had begun.

A few weeks after the conclusion of sex education, Mom gave my brother and me a book. She said she wanted us to read it and then ask her any questions we might have. My brother was in eighth grade; I figured at his age he already knew everything about sex. Instead, Mom seemed to think that a fifth-grade girl and an eighth-grade boy required comparable information.

*Where Did I Come From?* included colored illustrations, a larger-print font, and I was sure it was a picture book for a preschooler until I opened it. Inside was a google-eyed caricature of a boy standing on a high dive with an erection, a pool of girls waving at him from below. Another page illustrated a gaggle of girls with oddly sized breasts; the accompanying text explained that breast shapes are as unique as people. One page showed a group of salmon-colored sperm grinning at an egg with blue eyes and eyelashes, one hand on her hip. The sperm and egg appeared both friend and foe. I liked the idea that this new unfolding within my preteen body had a personality. It reminded me of Bugs Bunny and Garfield and the Chipmunks—Saturday morning cartoons that I hadn't watched in years. The facts of life seemed harmless and familiar.

* * *

I notice a brown spot in my underwear late Monday night. I am oddly calm when I call the doctor's office, as if I'm caught in some wind current and must simply stay the course. During the past two months, there have been countless trips to the bathroom, insatiable hunger, and tiredness that forces me to climb into bed at eight in the evening.

This is just another symptom of pregnancy.

The nurse tells me that brown spotting is okay—safe. She instructs me to put my feet up and relax. "Call us back if there are any changes or if you begin cramping."

I go upstairs and drop on the bed. Pete startles awake. He sits up straight, puts a hand on my arm and says, "What?"

Even in the dark I can see the wild, crazy panning of his eyes back and forth across my face. It makes me giggle. Then I tell him about the spotting.

"Are you okay?" He asks.

"I'm fine. The nurse said it's normal. There's nothing to worry about unless I start to cramp or it changes to bright red. We're safe."

I tell him to go back to sleep and position myself on the couch, feet up on a pillow, book in hand. I replay the conversation with the nurse. Try to relax. I get up every half hour and check my underpants. There's no change. We're safe.

\* \* \*

The following day, I wake in the darkness, stare out the window. Snow falls sideways, as if the angle helps it plummet faster. We've gotten six inches of snow overnight and they are predicting six more before noon. I make myself a cup of herbal tea, move right past the coffee pot that used to begin my morning routine. Everything changes in an instant. I wrap the teabag around a spoon, toss it in the garbage, and leave the cup on the counter.

In the bathroom I check my underwear. The same brown spotting. I am still not cramping. All the books say women frequently spot. That's what I'm doing. Spotting. As long as it's not bright red. As long as there's no cramping involved. My underwear is clean; but as I sit, four clumps of blood drop soundlessly out of me into the toilet—one, two, three, four. Maroon. Dark red. Reddish brown? The color. It has changed.

I call the doctor, take notes on the back of yesterday's *Chicago Tribune*, and then I call Pete. It isn't until I hear his voice on the other end of the line that mine falters.

\* \* \*

Dr. Murphy's nurse tells me to undress from the waist down. She hands me a folded paper sheet and tells me to drape myself with it. I take my place on the examining table and keep my socks on. They are black with gray stripes. Pete flips through a magazine. The TV in the corner plays *All My Children* and, for the first time, I see Eric, a boy I dated freshman year of high school. "I dated that guy," I point to the TV. "He broke up with me because I wouldn't sleep with him." He also once saved me when he knocked on the door of the hotel room where I'd been led by my Turnabout date.

Pete cranes his neck. "He looks like a Chachi," and changes the channel. This makes me smile. Pete's one of the few who still thinks Joanie from *Happy Days* should have never married Chachi.

When Dr. Murphy arrives, the jokes end. She squirts warm gel on my abdomen, runs the smooth head of the Doppler over my now sticky skin. Dr. Murphy can't find a heartbeat. "It might take a few minutes," she says repositioning the wand.

Every movement inside me is amplified. There are gurgles and dribbles, ticks and clunking, but no smooth, rapid-fire thrumming of an infant's heart. "This isn't unusual. Sometimes it's difficult to hear the heart at ten weeks." Was that it? Every noise sounds like a heartbeat, and I have to hold myself back from asking, *Was that the baby?*

I'm edgy, but not grim. Dr. Murphy orders blood work and an ultrasound in another office in a nearby town. Pete is quiet. I hate needles and dislike blood, but in the past few months I have learned to give myself over to those in white coats. This time a different nurse enters the exam room, knots the rubber band, and inserts the needle in my arm. As long as I don't see the blood eek out, I'm fine.

I look out the window at the piles of snow, flakes the size of popcorn, cars are—I jerk, look down at my extended arm. The syringe feels deeper than ever before and I worry that the needle may pop out the other side of the vein. The tube fills with dark blood. By the time we leave the office for the ultrasound, my forearm has blossomed into the green hillside of some faraway place.

The roads are slick with slush. The plows seem unable to keep up. They push sheets of wet snow, and just as quickly, the cleared paths fill and the heaps on the roadside tower. The dour sky tinges the snow pearly blue—an old woman's badly dyed hair, the high-heeled shoes my mother wore as a bridesmaid in her best friend's wedding, the powder room in the home where I grew up.

Pete turns the radio on. I dial down the volume. It takes ten minutes to travel a mile. The back tires spin, salt pebbles pling the car. Slush and ice accumulate on the windshield. Pete rolls down his window, grabs the wiper and lets it beat against the glass. Little chunks of ice skate across the windshield.

Tucked behind a row of overgrown, brick homes in the same shade of beige brick, the turnoff to the maternal fetal specialists is nearly concealed; there are two cars in the parking lot. A snow drift climbs up against the office door. Pete steps in front of me, swings the door back and forth, making a path. Inside, the walls are painted egg-yolk yellow, and one wall is lined with framed ultrasounds. I'm surprised by the clarity of these black-and-white images. Any ultrasound I've seen is grainy, blurred. Labels etched along the bottom list the age of each fetus.

"Hey, here's a ten-week one." I point to an image and both of us take a step forward. I can see the face with its crunched eyelids, arms extending from shoulders, a glimpse of neck. I grab Pete around the waist, hug him. We're going to see our baby!

When I was young, I thought that if you wanted to become a mother, you needed to tell God how many children you desired. Once I held up four fingers in the air for a whole night. I don't share this with Pete, atheist as he is, but I think about the intervening years as I investigate the rest of the photos. The youngest fetus on the wall is seven weeks old with an oblong head and tail. *The doctors here can help me*, I think.

We take our seats and watch a very pregnant woman and her mother make their way down the hallway. I root through the stack of magazines but there are only multiple copies of the same issue—a magazine for mothers-to-be ages thirty-five and older, the age I'll be next year. I try to maintain the excitement I felt while looking at the pictures on the wall, although something else has arrived. The tiniest twinge of a cramp.

The room the technician ushers us into is no larger than a walk-in closet. The lights are off, but the glossy screen tipped near the ceiling takes up much of the room, reminding me of the planetarium. The technician asks why we're here. It seems like such an odd question. Surely the orders Dr. Murphy sent over explained our appointment. But this question is another test that I must pass. I tell her that I experienced some spotting the previous day and that earlier today, Dr. Murphy had been unable to find a heartbeat. "How far along are you?" she asks.

"I'll be eleven weeks this Thursday." When she asks me about cramping, I look her in the eye and say I don't have any.

She instructs me to lie down on the table, to unbutton my jeans. I pull my shirt up and she pours warm gel onto my stomach. She turns on the computer in front of her, clicks a few buttons, and the screen hums to life. This is the first time Pete has been with me for an ultrasound, and I want him to see me confident of each step.

When she waves the wand over the lower part of my abdomen the cool wetness brings to mind Ban, the roll-on deodorant my parents used to share. An image appears on the screen. I hold on to the ends of my shirt, wait for the technician to talk. She shifts the wand, taps a few keys on her computer, clicks the mouse, and freezes the image.

I stare intently. Squint. I'm not sure what I see.

"What's that?"

"I'm not the one who does the talking," she says. "I just take the pictures."

She tells me that she'd like to take another ultrasound now, one that will allow us to see inside me from a different angle. I'm instructed to take off my jeans and underwear and return to the table. The technician tells me to bend my knees, and I watch her squirt K-Y on a phallic-looking tube that she inserts inside me. She drapes a sheet over my knees and returns to her computer. The room is eerily quiet except for her tapping on the keyboard.

There's a new image on the screen. A circle with rippled edges. The technician who doesn't want to answer my questions puts her hands between my legs and shifts the tube, clicks the mouse. Tap tap, click. The images that she takes line up, until black-and-white boxes fill the screen.

Something lodges in my throat, obstructs my breathing, and I can't take in all the air that I need. I tremble from the waist up.

A man in a white coat enters the room. I startle. I'm not wearing any pants and the sheet has crept up to my thighs. But the man in the white coat doesn't seem interested in me. He looks at the computer screen, barks orders at the technician.

I wonder what his name is.

Under his direction, the technician begins to click on some of the boxes on the screen. "I don't see anything," says the man in the white coat. He is animated. He waves both hands in front of him like he might gesture that he is finished with his dinner, ready for the bill. "I'm sorry."

I do not understand. I look from him to the screen. Something in these boxes has excited him. The fact that we are here, waiting for him to speak, seems to anger him. He keeps waving his arms, and if I were closer, he might hit me.

He tells the technician to run a certain test and a rainbow of colors ripple over the screen, a wave of friendly brightness in this dark, hushed room. And then the man in the white coat speaks again about the projected images. "It's not even a nice, smooth shape. I'm sorry." He walks out, shuts the door behind him. I still don't know his name.

I count. Sixteen images in all. The technician pulls the tube out from between my legs and the black-and-white photos remain lined up on the screen. "So, you understand everything the doctor said."

This is a statement, not a fact, nor question.

"I don't know." My knees are still bent; Pete puts a hand on my shoulder. "I guess," but I don't. I don't know what he said, why he waved his hands like that. Where's the baby?

"This will be considered a miscarriage," she said. *Oh no.* Everything inside me crumbles and I want to leave the room, I want to be alone, but my pants are off and I'm stretched out on a table and there is nowhere to go.

Fingers—the five on each hand press into my eyelids. A door shuts and Pete puts his arms around me, tries to hold me, but my knees are bent. They will not straighten. This is the position for an ultrasound; this is how you see the fetus.

*Please. Please look at me*, he says. I shake my head, *no*.

\* \* \*

The day before the D&C, I am wrapped in an afghan on the couch. I'm trying to figure out why my body rebelled. Was it the X-ray machine at the Reagan National Airport? Did I swim too hard, not take my pulse accurately? Never a milk drinker, I drank a glass every night before bed. But maybe I shouldn't have veered from my milkless diet. I stopped using the cream for the rash on my wrist as soon as I realized I was pregnant, but the medicine could have still been in my system. I banged my head on the trunk of the car while loading my carry-on after the work trip to Washington DC—did the trauma of that bruise somehow end this pregnancy?

Mom is spending the day battling the snow—we've gotten a foot in less than eight hours and she is determined to keep her driveway clear. Between shoveling, she calls me on the phone, reminds me to trust in the Lord. Yet I fear this too. Despite twelve years of Catholic schooling, I am far from religious.

Did God take this baby from us?

\* \* \*

The bloody clumps are hot and slick. They arrive in thick, irregularly shaped masses and are accompanied by stomach pains unlike any I've ever experienced. When they seize me, I double over, drop to the floor, and curl up onto my side. Breathing takes work. I take in short, stumpy breaths, exhale through my mouth.

The pain comes in waves every few minutes. I make fists. Tears and snot drop off. There is a war waging within and I am only a bystander. I position Pete's shaving mirror between my legs so that I can catch the blobs, bring them to the hospital tomorrow. I've already filled three Ziplock bags when I see her: a one-inch-tall nub of flesh with four buds—two arms, two legs. In our black-and-white tiled bathroom with the yellow painted walls, I hold her in my palm.

\* \* \*

My nurse's name is Sheryl. Her fizzy brown hair hangs below her shoulders and her earrings are loops made of turquoise beads. *She probably vacations in Arizona or New Mexico*, I am thinking, when she says in a petaled voice, "I am so sorry for your loss."

In the operating room, Sheryl helps me onto a long table. As I stretch out, the cramps spread and lengthen until the ache extends from end to end. She pulls the cotton gown from underneath me so that my bare backside presses against the table. Once they give me the anesthesia, they'll strip off this thin gown and I won't even know it. Sheryl stands at my right, taps my hand, tells me I'm going to be just fine. The anesthesiologist is behind my head. He tells me he likes my socks—they're black with brown, red, and blue flecks. I look down at them and wiggle my toes. What begins as a thought in my head becomes true through my body. I am surprised at the innocence of this tiny motion. "Thanks," I tell him. "I was just thinking I need to buy more socks."

This makes them laugh, and it holds on a second too long. Later I realize this laughter is their condolence.

I wake in a quick instant. The cramps, the ache—all of it gone. I'm back in my hospital room. Pete is here. Dr. Murphy tells me everything went well, that she'll give me a prescription for an antibiotic; she says she wants to see me in her office next week. She tells Pete to keep an eye on me, pats my leg, and turns to leave. But the idea of her leaving makes me panic. "The doctor at the ultrasound—"

She turns back around and my tears begin to run hot and fast. I try to mimic the way he tossed his arm in front of him to gesture nothing—no viable fetus, no life, but my arm is weighed by the IV, grogginess. "I deserve to know the truth. Miscarriage. He didn't use the word and that's what it was. I deserve the truth."

Dr. Murphy tells Sheryl to get me a Kleenex, and Sheryl dries my cheeks.

"You're the second person this week to complain about him." Dr. Murphy rests a hand on my leg, promises to speak with him, then disappears.

"Shh, it's okay," says Pete, wiping my tears with his fingers. Something inside me loosens. I close my eyes for a minute and open them again. Someone's opened the curtains. Sunlight streams in. In it, I notice the slow descent of dust. The snow is out there, only I can't see it. There is a postage-sized stamp of sky, a vivid blue, the color of a summer day well in the future, a time when anything seems possible. Pete spoons a chip of ice into my mouth. Nothing has ever tasted so good.

\* \* \*

*Well, there was obviously something wrong. Wouldn't you rather it happens now than when the baby is born? Don't worry, you'll get pregnant again.*

When I tell a family member about the miscarriage and mention my fear that I might not be able to have a child, she asks, "Well, can you?"

People are well meaning. They don't know what to say and feel they must say something. I know that they want to carry the burden in some way, offer words that will make things better. Yet grief is an entirely personal experience.

Now four weeks later, when Pete returns from work to find me on the couch, sitting, he reaches for my hand, takes a seat beside me. "How are you?" he asks, looking into my face as if the answer is written there. I shrug my shoulders. Pete has told me he doesn't think about the pregnancy. He has worked through his pain.

We sit in the stillness. Finally, I find the words. "I'm feeling sad today." There are no signs or directions to explain how to get from this sadness to who and what was before. That path is unnavigable. I can only move forward from this unfamiliar place. The time before now is over.

# THE SACRED DISEASE

Living in Indiana, our lives have an agrarian bent. In June, we pick strawberries at Annie's and make a double batch of jam. I let our twin daughters, Eva and Jolie, sit on the counter, a giant bowl between them. They will be four in the fall and they take turns crushing berries with a potato masher while the other holds the rim. In July, we hang pails from the belts of our pants as we pick blueberries at Martin Acres. The girls peer into my bucket, ask me how I picked them so fast, and then grab handfuls to throw into their own pails. But later, the laughter recedes when we are in our kitchen and Eva is begging, crying, reaching toward the pre-dinner cookie I won't let her have. Suddenly she stills, looks up at me, mouth ajar. No sounds escape.

"Eva!"

I grab her at the waist and pick her up. A second or two passes and her head slumps onto my shoulder. Her arms and legs clench forward, and my three-year-old daughter rocks with convulsions, seizing me in her grip. Eva clenches her jaw and grates her teeth. As her head jerks, I softly say, "Mommy's here. Come back to Mommy." I hold her as tight as I am able. "Mommy loves you. It's okay," I say, to both of us. She releases her bladder and I welcome the warm flood of her insides. Her eyes dart back and forth beneath the half-mast of her eyelids. That's how I know she's still seizing.

Her body is not yet her own.

\* \* \*

Aunt Sandy took barbiturates for her seizures but always seemed to forget them before a holiday gathering. One Thanksgiving both my grandmas, my mom's brother and his wife, my cousins, all of us were seated around folding tables we'd arranged in a large rectangle in our wood-paneled basement. Pilgrims posed on paper tablecloths and earlier we had helped Mom make centerpieces of gourds and ornamental corn, red globe grapes, for color. Maybe I was eating my stuffing or on my second helping of cranberries—I only recall the clink of silverware, someone screaming. "Sandy!" When I looked up, I saw Aunt Sandy slumped to one side in her chair, arms jerking rapidly, eyes slitted and unfocused.

"Sandy!" My grandma scolded, voice booming amid the sudden silence, "You forgot to take your medicine!" Mom sprang into action. She slid Aunt Sandy out of her folding chair and onto the rug, put her on her side as her chin twisted into the ground, knees clenched up, arms shuddering. Her shirt had ridden up, exposing a white band of flesh; a dark pool soiled her slacks.

Mom patted her arms, remained at her side, cooed, "It's okay. You're all right."

A line existed between where the makeup on Aunt Sandy's face ended and her neck began. I stood there and held my arms. Didn't know what to do. "It's okay, Sandy," said Mom. She kept a hand on Aunt Sandy's hip as she continued to seize, never let her hand veer from my aunt's body.

I waited for a moment when the adults wouldn't be watching and I could slip upstairs to my bedroom and call one of my friends. It was all so disgusting. The lack of control Aunt Sandy had for her body seemed connected to her polyester pants and the one-room apartment she rented next to Shaky's Pizza, the avocado carpeting leading to her door flattened into the shape of footprints. Inside, her parakeet scattered bits of birdseed and scat in his cage as his penciled feet pricked bar to bar.

When it was over, Aunt Sandy snored. Great sobs of breath racketed her body right there on our basement rug; the moon of her back rose and fell. Mom covered her with the afghan we used while we watched TV. For weeks afterward the blanket remained in a heap beside the couch like some diseased animal whose sickness we feared catching.

* * *

Eva has seized in the hospital, at the neighborhood park next door, in our kitchen, her bedroom, our bathroom, on the living room floor in the summer, while she was fighting a cold in the winter, and once on Mother's Day as I was hoisting her from her high chair. Her first seizure occurred when she was thirteen months old and we were living in Philadelphia.

We tried anti-seizure medication for a few years, but our already quiet daughter became quieter, her speech further delayed. Instead, we rely on Diastat, a pre-filled syringe with medicine that can halt a seizure. The major side effect of it is that it also suppresses her respiration. Every Diastat application has ended with a trip to the hospital.

I keep Diastat vials in our kitchen cabinet below the shelf with the cookbooks. Two vials are in my purse; another vial near the glasses, and later, there will be two vials in the preschool classroom where Eva will spend Monday and Tuesday mornings.

Before she attended preschool, her three teachers visited our home to meet Eva and Jolie. While the girls crouched on the floor with their Dora figurines, the teachers asked me if there was anything I'd like to tell them. Only then did I remove the Diastat from its paper bag, break the seal on its plastic carrier, and take out the syringe.

I passed it to each teacher and explained that if Eva had a seizure that lasted more than two minutes, they needed to administer the Diastat. I told them how to place her on her side on the floor, pull down her pants, bend one leg forward, dip the syringe into the lubricating jelly, and then insert it into Eva's rectum while counting to three. After plunging the syringe and holding her rectum closed, count to three again, and then remove the syringe. I asked them to hold Eva as they waited for the paramedics to arrive.

The lead teacher opened her mouth in either shock or fear—I'm not sure which. A spackle of spit stretched the corner of her lips. I waited for her to say that she was sorry, that perhaps another school would be a better choice for our breath-holding daughter.

Instead, the teachers slid onto their knees and shook the girls' hands, told them they looked forward to seeing them in preschool. I swiped my wet eyes, overfilled with gratitude.

\* \* \*

The Babylonians once considered seizures punishment for some wrongdoing or sin, as revealed on tablets dating back to 2000 BC that list several types of seizures, each of which is associated with the name of an evil spirit or god. It wasn't until Hippocrates published *The Sacred Disease* in the fifth century BC that he debunked the idea of epilepsy being some scourge on a soul, declaring it a brain disorder instead. He didn't believe "that a human could be invaded by a god, the basest by the most pure." He recommended physical treatments, and even surgery, and stated only if the disease became chronic was it incurable.

Early treatments for epilepsy advocated by Hippocrates include surgical blood letting or skull trephination, in which a hole is drilled into the skull to remove bone. Still, those who experienced seizures were also often thought to be possessed and were confined to special groups or shunned altogether. Initially, people with epilepsy tended to live in poorhouses, state institutions, or crowded jails. The Ohio Hospital for Epileptics, established in 1893, was the first seizure colony in the United States. There, treatments included special diets and hydro therapeutics—hot and cold baths. At the same time, there was a growing acceptance of eugenics. It was thought that children who were "defective"—those who suffered from seizures, but also those who were poor, feebleminded, or sexually promiscuous—should be segregated during their "entire reproductive lives" to restrict increase of "their kind."

\* \* \*

Aunt Sandy lost her son David to Lake Michigan when he was sixteen years old. Her husband had died of a heart attack a few years prior. She'd raised David alone with the help of her two sisters, my grandma and aunt. Of the sisters, Aunt Sandy was the pretty one with her blonde curls, laughter as light as cotton candy.

David had been at the beach in South Chicago with his friends. He'd never been a strong swimmer, but he and his friends waded out, goofed around like any other group of teenagers. It was toward the end of summer and I imagine it was a hot day, sun glinting the lake like blades. There were girls nearby they were supposedly eyeing. As they waded deeper, the heavy fabric of his swim trunks billowed with the force of each wave.

He wasn't tall, but girls found him cute and he liked flirting. Most of what I know about that day comes from my grandma: the girls, the beach, his friends, the drowning. He picked out the best-looking girl of the bunch, held her tightly in his sight, grinned. I'd like to think he thought about jokes he'd offer, things he might say once he was on land.

So, I imagine the tide pushed him further, his friends suddenly far away, laughing about something. *What's so funny*, he thought. He dug his toes downward, searched for the sandbar. It had been there all along. He swept his legs from side to side, searching. Then harder, kicking his feet in every direction, twisting his torso—where was it? The bottom was gone.

He punched the surface. Grew disoriented. Something rammed his throat. He could still hear some far-off crackle of conversation. Where were his friends?

A wave pummeled him.

As he swallowed water and flapped his arms, his mother was at work, canning soup at the Campbell's Chicago plant. But he didn't have time to consider her. She didn't see him struggle to keep his chin up, hands two useless knobs of splash. She did not look up from a blanket on the shore, scan the horizon, and glimpse the oval of his forehead disappear.

They say that Aunt Sandy was different after David's death. More distant—spacey. My grandma used to take my siblings and me to visit her at the McDonald's in Calumet City. She worked the fryer, dropped baskets of french fries into vats of oil that snapped at her skin, left tiny red spots on her wrists. She wore a paper cone hat, a navy polyester jumper with a zipper down the front. My grandma would write our order on a hand-sized tablet before leaving her house: Quarter Pounders with extra pickles, small soft drinks without ice, fries. We never called out to Aunt Sandy while she worked, but quietly took our lunches to a table with attached swivel chairs and ate. Later, she would walk up with a broom and a dustpan and brush the crumbs from beneath our feet. Sometimes she would go back behind the counter and talk with her manager and he would let her go on break. She'd sit beside my grandma with a Styrofoam cup of coffee. They'd both take off the lids, let the steam escape as they chatted, Aunt Sandy's voice as hollow as a plastic toy.

* * *

Sometimes children can have breath-holding spells during which time their oxygen drops so low that they pass out. On rare occasions, they can have seizures. Young children have a lower threshold for seizures than adults, which is why many childhood epilepsies are outgrown. Breath holding usually runs in families, and my mother can recall my brother at age two having a temper tantrum so severe that he held his breath and passed out. But he did not seize.

If Eva's seizures truly are caused by breath holding rather than a neurological condition, her neurologist believes she will grow out of them sometime between the ages of four and six. If not, she will be diagnosed with a seizure disorder. And that will bring with it its own challenges. She may not be allowed to drive or play certain sports. Or maybe she'll just be a little different, like Aunt Sandy. But I get ahead of myself. It's easy to do.

* * *

The first thing Eva does when a seizure ends is cry. One long fanged sob that comes from some place deep inside her—it sounds crooked and unbalanced. It is the cry of an older woman. Aunt Sandy, perhaps. The echo of her long-ago agony, returning from work that summer day to find her house empty, a line of police cars outside her door, lights flashing but soundless.

Aunt Sandy never talked about David, but she kept a framed picture of him on a hall table where I liked to linger. In his high school photo, David's cheeks were dimpled and he had his mother's good looks, the kind that would've aged well, thick wavy hair, cerulean eyes.

How often did Aunt Sandy put her head down at night and return to that day dreaming that she powered through the waves as if parting them, lifting David onto her hip and into the air to breathe, then fixing him to her side as she pulled them both to shore?

Or maybe in her dreams she was on the bed in the delivery room, bearing his weight for the last time.

But no—that was me.

They let me labor twenty-two hours when the doctor announced that it was time. The amniotic fluid around Eva was dropping and they needed to do a C-section. In the OR, they helped me onto a table, injected anesthesia between the knots of my spine and told me to hurry and stretch out as everything from my waist down numbed within seconds. The room filled. There were two teams of doctors, one for each baby. There must have been fifteen-some people milling about in blue scrubs.

My husband, Pete, was near my head. They placed a screen just below my collarbone, so I couldn't see anything. But I couldn't stop smiling. Pete had already begun tearing up, moving nonexistent hair off my forehead and leaning over to kiss me. "How can you be so calm?" he asked.

"I just am."

I asked him to tell me what was taking place on the other side of the drape, but he wouldn't remove his eyes from mine. He was touching my face when the doctor announced, "It's a girl!" and then I heard Eva's red-throated cry. Two minutes later, the doctor announced Jolie's arrival.

Later, in our hospital room, we opened the blankets the nurses wrapped them in and counted their toes and fingers. We used our hands, which already looked so clunky and imperfect next to the girls', to memorize the stems of their arms and legs. I didn't say it, but I thought it: *I am going to keep you safe.*

\* \* \*

There is a safety to holding Eva as she seizes, to serve as witness.

I can support the lolling head. I can catch the wayward limbs. I can watch her eyes slip back and forth without destination, just left and right, a novice waltz. Afterward I can rock her in my arms. I can hold her as she sleeps. I can wipe her clean and dress her in dry clothes. But time passes.

Someday she will be in a car driving on a nameless highway. Someday she will have a crush she will lean forward to kiss, her breath hemmed in expectation; someday she might be at the beach, sunning herself with friends. She might enter the surf in hopes of cooling off and her breath might halt—the familiar spasms recognizing the foamy peals, the relentless turning over of water like breath itself; one wave followed by another.

* * *

A week after Eva's initial seizure and hospitalization in Philadelphia, she still wore a faint red strip from the tape they'd put on her face when they intubated her, but it was fading, and I was hopeful.

We'd had a good day. I'd taken the girls to the park that morning and after a lunch of their favorite dumplings from Trader Joe's, the girls perched on mini pink gingham armchairs while I sat cross-legged between them reading *The Bear Snores On* or *Jamberry*, books that caused them to grin as they pointed to the pages. The girls were a little over a year old and that day, after closing our last book, I announced it was time to nap. I picked up Jolie and headed to the girls' bedroom with her.

As I walked the wood floors, the early afternoon brightness, Eva began to holler. "I'll be right back," I told her, my skin prickling. "I'm going to put Sissy in her crib and then I'll be right back."

But Eva had already begun crying. Her face fisted tight, that sudden reddening. I could have put Jolie down and picked Eva up. It's what she wanted. Instead, I curled my arm tighter around Jolie. "We'll be right back," I pleaded, legs beginning to tremble.

I took a few more steps and Eva followed me, her arms outstretched. "Please," I said, my words wobbly. "Just let me put your sister in her crib."

Jolie would have been fine if I'd put her down, but I didn't want to. Jolie smiled and laughed quickly. And unlike her sister, she didn't hold her breath. She didn't have seizures.

I was now behind the couch and still held Jolie just a few feet from their bedroom door when I turned around, faced the room's sudden quiet. Eva was on the other side of the couch, near the seat cushions. I could see her face, her eyes glassy, mouth open, but no sound, and then she dropped away and was no longer upright, but on the floor, arms and legs jerking, jerking.

I put Jolie aside and scooped Eva into my arms, my own limbs blocky and rigid, mouth papery, and then it all came back to me, the sounds from just a week ago—the screeching ambulance making its way down 21st Street on its way to the Children's Hospital of Philadelphia, the bank of windows in our third-floor apartment reflecting my own sorrowful face.

"I'm sorry," I said, thinking of Eva in the hospital bed with the tiny green gown that snapped at the shoulders, nodes stuck to her thin chest. I'm sorry, I thought, counted one thousand one. One thousand two. I went over in my mind the steps to administer the Diastat, remembered how immediately after Eva's hospital discharge, we drove to the CVS on Walnut Street and when the pharmacist said it would take two or three days for the Diastat to arrive, I began to cry, the pharmacist, his kind expression, "I'm sorry," he said. And meant it.

I'm sorry, I told Eva. I'm sorry.

* * *

Status epilepticus, the life-threatening seizure Eva initially experienced, carries with it a high rate of mortality and neurologic deficits.

"You know we almost lost her," Pete said once. "We almost left Philadelphia as a family of three."

I don't know what the future holds for Eva. Her seizures are growing less frequent and when they do happen, they are shorter in duration. We're trying to teach her to verbalize her frustration rather than hold her breath. Some days are better than others. But at the park beside our house, I train myself for whatever is yet to come. If Eva is hanging on the bars, swinging her legs back and forth, I watch her from the cement walk, a few feet away. When she is on the swing, begging to go higher, I push her. Her curls spring in the air and she grins, says, "Higher, Mommy. Higher!" I push her, note the solid grip of her hands on the chains—she flies.

I let her go.

# VINEGAR

Fridays I clean. I begin by flipping the kitchen chairs upside down on the table, taking the bin of newspapers from the place near the couch and balancing it in the rungs of one of the upended chairs. I do the same with the crate of dog toys, and then make sure there aren't any unforeseen ponytail holders or Legos lingering beneath the couch. Our ninety-pound lab-shepherd mix sheds, so the first step is to vacuum. I prefer to do it right. I pick the flattened pads of dog hair that stick to the bottoms of the chairs, and then I fill a bucket with hot water and a generous amount of vinegar.

There's only one way to clean floors: on hands and knees. Bent at the waist, reaching beneath the lip of the cabinets, running a rag on the baseboard, the vinegar catches the splattered spaghetti sauce and the sand the girls brought in from the backyard sandbox. I scrub a dried green bit and assume it's lettuce or broccoli and move on.

Pete thought I was insane when he discovered me on hands and knees on the floor of our Cleveland apartment during our first year of marriage. I didn't try and persuade him on this long-standing method, I just went on with my work. The floors of our Indiana home, where we live now, are hardwood everywhere except the kitchen and bath, both of which respond nicely to vinegar. Still, despite the grime the dog or our daughters trample in, it's the floors that concern me. No matter what freelance deadline I've got on my plate or student work that begs a response, I've got to clean the floors or something in me feels unsettled.

All the women in my family swear by vinegar. We use it to clean our floors and sour the tomato sauce that simmers around our cabbage rolls. It cleans windows streak-free and even removes chlorine from hair. We discovered this thanks to Mrs. Derbue, Mom's friend who cut our hair as kids and permed Mom's in her basement's makeshift salon. We swam competitively and each time we went for a trim, Mrs. Derbue rubbed the strands of our hair between her fingers, mouth puckered in disgust. But once we began to squirt our heads with vinegar and water, then followed this with shampoo, Mrs. Derbue announced our hair much improved. I couldn't feel the chlorine build up, but I liked the satisfaction of eliminating something unnatural.

* * *

As a child, weekends were spent camping. My parents were proud to say they paid cash for our 1978 Starcraft pop-up. Dad had accepted a new job and they used his pay increase to buy the camper. When we arrived at a campground Mom would help Dad back into the site, and then Dad would unhitch the car, fit a crank into the camper's frame, and with each turn the canvas walls unfurled. The lid of the camper rose until it became the ceiling. It took two of us to pull out the plywood bunks—and it was my responsibility to fasten the support poles beneath each bunk.

Dad and Michael blocked the front and back of each tire with a chunk of wood, and then hooked up the electricity and water by fastening two feet of severed hose to the side of the camper, letting this drain into an old paint bucket. Mom says now that camping was a way to feel like we were vacationing despite the fact that we didn't have money for extravagance. Meals were prepared on a charcoal fire. Hobo dinners were a favorite—squares of tinfoil pocketed with a beef patty, slices of potatoes, onions, tomatoes and zucchini, a dash of salt, pepper, and half a cube of beef bouillon. During thunderstorms, we huddled around the Formica table that collapsed to form the base of Michael's bed and ate bowls of chili with Saltines, or spaghetti and meatballs that Mom would bring in a Tupperware from home, white blocks of ice crusting around hunks of meat. Rain beat the canvas walls in a dull hum. The fabric flapped as trees shook their leaves, flung down twigs and sometimes branches.

In those days, I thought my parents knew everything—they could drive, set up a portable home on wheels, feed my siblings and me tasty food. But only now do I realize my good fortune—the color of my skin, my parents' education, the fact that they were still together. They were as uncertain of the way forward as every parent. Exhausted at the end of the night, worrying about paying our tuition at the Catholic school, wondering if they could stomach another season with their bosses, fearful this might be the year our basement sump pump would fail.

No matter where we went, my parents always brought along a blue train case filled with pills and bandages, bottles of Dimetap for sore throats and Donagel, which tasted like chalky bananas, for upset stomachs. The train case had been a wedding gift and when opened the silky blue lining gave off the faint scent of Coppertone. The inside pocket looked like a garter with its gathered folds. Maybe during their honeymoon Mom had used such a pocket to hold a fancy nightgown. But growing up, it became our portable medicine cabinet. When one of us were ill, if they decided something could be remedied without a visit to our pediatrician, they'd open the train case and sort through the bottles and pills.

In the haze of a fever, sticky with fatigue and slumped in my bed or on the corner of the couch, I'd hear them open the train case. "Carl, should we start her on something?"

"I don't know, Judy. Try the amoxicillin." And, moments later, I'd hear him uncorking the childproof cap from a bottle of powdered medicine, mixing this with sterilized water from a jug, then shaking this until it formed a thin pink liquid that tasted as candied as the color pink looked. When Mom approached me in my bed holding the plastic medicine dispenser, she would ask me to sit up and then put an arm around me, maybe cup my shoulder. She looked both concerned and deeply interested, like I was a puzzle worth solving. I'd sit in her deep gaze, throat flaming, maybe sticky with sweat as she held the dispenser to my mouth and told me to drink all of it. A wave of contentment would drop over me and everything shifted: the sheets on my feet softened, caressed my legs with a cool touch; the ticking of the closed shades in the open window, a bird far off sweetly trilling.

Everything about Mom seemed so sure and impenetrable. I don't remember thinking that I, too, would one day become a mother, but at some point, I must have made the connection because my fifth-grade journal includes a list at the back with the header "Notes to Myself When I am a Mom."

"Wear fashionable clothes!" The first note says. And another—"sidewalk painting: water + food coloring + paintbrushes make an easy outdoor activity for kids." If only parenthood had been as easy as figuring out how to keep kids entertained.

* * *

Maybe Pete and I would have had more children if we'd married earlier, although we are fortunate to have our daughters. I didn't have a problem getting pregnant; holding onto the pregnancies proved more difficult. With my first pregnancy, we had been trying for a few months and I had been reading books and blogs about conception signs, so when I woke in the middle of the night with cramps, I knew it was implantation. By the time I finally bought a drugstore test, the plus sign was a mere formality. I couldn't have been more elated. Suddenly everything had purpose—a bite of orange, a sip of milk. Everything I did or ate held greater meaning.

I read *What to Expect When You're Expecting* three or more times a day, memorizing the illustrations, noticing how the fetus's bulbous eyes moved closer together with each week, the dome head narrowing, growing round. I scrutinized drawings at seven weeks as hands and feet began to develop. At eight weeks eyelids appeared. Nine weeks the long fish-like tail shrunk to a stump and split to form two leg buds. And by week ten, when I began to spot, the illustration looked like a human fetus. I called the nurse as soon as the splotches darkened the toilet bowl.

A long, cold winter followed. I remember curling up on the sofa uninterested in reading or writing, eating, talking, or existing. We planted a white bud near the front of our house. I watched how a strong wind pushed the branches against the windows, made them bend but not break.

During the second miscarriage we'll be living in Philadelphia with our sixteen-month-old twin daughters, who were determined to climb everything—the couch, an empty box, the rails of their cribs. Mom will fly in from Chicago to help. The night before the D&C, I'll take her to a favorite coffee shop for gelato and we'll walk the narrow-cobbled roads as streetlights blink on, the sun dipping behind high rises. She'll drive me to the hospital for the surgery on those same narrow streets. Afterward, I'll wake nauseous, unable to hold my head upright.

During my last miscarriage, we'll be in Indiana. The technician will tuck a towel into my underwear, squirt cool gel onto my abdomen and run a wand over this. I'll follow along with the technician's movements on an overhead screen that fills the wall, magnifies my insides a trillion times. The heart rate will already be outside a healthy range and that weekend I'll sip a glass of wine with a good friend, certain this pregnancy also will not take.

But the first miscarriage will remain the most vivid. Hours after the spots of blood, I bled actively, passed thick clots. Every month, for twenty-some years my body had shed this lining, this possibility. I felt that this child had glimpsed something inside me and turned away. A lifetime of darkness and mistakes churned inside me, a great inhospitable gloom.

I squatted over the toilet as the wave of each cramp clenched down, kneaded my stomach, dug both fists inside, and tried to clamp down on the pain. Heavy clumps slid from me and I caught a piece of warm matter in my palm, a human tadpole—faceless and unnamed.

It will take years before I stop thinking I could have prevented the miscarriage in some way. When it happened to Mom they were living in Madison, Wisconsin, where Dad was a graduate student, his sideburns pork chop thick. Mom's doctor told her to bring the pieces she passed to the hospital so that they could determine whether she miscarried the entire fetus; but during the second one she remained at home, like me, overseeing her own mutiny.

\* \* \*

Mom and I went to the Museum of Science and Industry in Chicago two weeks before that initial miscarriage. The elementary school where she worked as a nurse had closed for a holiday and I took a day off from my editorial job. That morning I shared news with her of my pregnancy. I handed her the picture of the ultrasound and she squealed, "You mean, I'm going to have a grandchild?" She hugged me hard and fast.

We had tickets to see Body Worlds, an exhibit by Gunther von Hagens, a German scientist who discovered a method for halting decomposition to preserve once-live specimens—human and animal—which he dissected and then shaped into lifelike poses. There was a horse in mid-leap with a jockey perched on his back. The dissected horse was composed of taut red muscles, which upon closer inspection showed striated muscle fibers and ligaments, white chunks of fat, and ropy tendons. The jockey on his back was spliced into thirds—the front of his face and body, the midsection full of inner organs and the pearly gleam of bone made up the backside as he held fast to the reins.

There was a family of four out for a day at the park, their skinned selves a panoply of bones and muscles and tendons. White globed eyeballs and fleshy lips delighted at the excursion. The mom held their picnic inside a wicker basket. The boy carried a Frisbee and darted ahead while we examined their anatomical structures.

Mom and I jostled between the other exhibit-goers and when I grew tired, I sat on a bench. I was only eight weeks along, but I could already feel the changes inside my body—the increasing thirst, the not-right hunger that filled me, how I craved food but eating left me feeling as if I might vomit.

The Body Worlds exhibit had been sold out for weeks and we were fortunate to secure tickets, but I was more eager to travel to the third floor of the museum, where I had a faint memory of an exhibit of fetuses. Sure enough, in a darkened room, beside the exhibit of a giant-sized plastic heart you could walk through, were a semi-circle of twenty-four real human embryos and fetuses in glass blocks. They ranged in age from six weeks to a whopping thirty-nine, the latter crammed so tight that I could see the fuzz of facial hair on her chin.

A single light shone on each fetus. I held a hand to my stomach as I approached the first display. The first, at six weeks, appeared no larger than a pea. By nine weeks, the fetus had transformed into a kidney bean, the oversized head unfurling, umbilical a dangling wisp. I moved onto the thirteen-week-old fetus, where its fish-like features had disappeared and it had begun to take up space, filling the middle of the block. It had fingers, hands, lips. Its eyelids were closed, fat just beginning to pad her elbows and thighs. I lost track of Mom. Swallowed. A brief sign at the start of the exhibit noted that all of the fetuses were donated in 1939 and that they had perished of natural causes, a result of the Great Depression. A doctor from a local hospital who had secured the parents' permission had obtained these specimens. The fetuses had been entombed like this for more than seventy years. The parents long gone, I supposed, but here, in the dark with only the illuminated tombs, a hallowed sense overcame me, a low murmur of guests accompanied me as I made my way along the line of fetuses, arms held tight.

\* \* \*

When I became pregnant with our daughters, my doctor prescribed progesterone, a hormone that the body naturally produces during pregnancy. Around eight o'clock each night, Pete washed his hands and drew up the medicine while I held a pack of ice to my backside. We did this for twelve weeks and it gradually became routine. During that same period, I was scheduled to attend a work conference in New Orleans. I invited Mom to join me so she could help administer the progesterone. She scrubbed her hands, then carefully drew the injection into the eight-gauge needle, her reading glasses perched at the end of her nose. I stretched out on the hotel bed; pants pulled to the side. I don't remember us talking about what it was like for her to help me in this way, but I wonder now what thoughts came to mind. As a nurse, she respected medicine and its accompanying regimens. I wonder if she thought of her own unborn children, the two miscarriages she endured. It isn't something we've ever discussed. Yet this loss is something we've shared.

\* \* \*

On Fridays when I wash the floors with vinegar, it all returns to me. This is where Eva released her bladder with her last seizure. This is where Pete drops his bags each day he returns from work. This is where last month Jolie walked into the counter, the blood streaking fast down her forehead. This is where we stood talking about our neighbor with stage-four pancreatic cancer, his bland yellow skin foreshadowing his eventual passing.

I do the bathrooms next, scrubbing the toilets and sinks, Windex the glass in the shower stall, clean the dried saliva off the windows where the dog stands, barking at the neighbor's cat. There are cobwebs in certain corners of the walls. I'll see them randomly on a Tuesday and swat it with the back of my hand, then wipe this on my jeans or just take the crumbled web and drop it in the garbage. Dirt and dust accumulate.

There are other things I could be doing with my time: a class to prep for, workshop stories to read, laundry that demands folding. Yet when I am on hands and knees dunking an old burp cloth into a bucket of vinegar water, then swiping this on the place where my daughter spilled her milk, really scrubbing it, I feel progress. The back and forth of the damp rag, dropping it in the bucket, swishing it around a few times then picking it back up, twisting out the excess into the gray water that stills the bucket. I think of my mother and her mother on their knees, washing their own floors, hands pruned by the hot water, vinegar permeating their skin. I wonder what occupied their minds as they worked. I imagine my grandma worrying about what would happen when my grandpa noticed the empty bottle of scotch, the contents of which she had dumped into the sink. Perhaps Mom perseverated upon the harsh words of a fellow swim team parent or tried to figure out how to sew a costume for the school play, maybe wondered if she had enough potatoes for stew or if she needed to run to the store before her hospital shift. After finishing their floors, both of them would sit back on her heels and inspect her work.

Most of my friends pay for someone to clean their homes. Even my friend Emily has a woman who comes to her condo each month with a bucket and rags, various bottles of cleaning agents. We had a cleaning lady for a few months when we moved to Indiana. Pete became ill and my constitution was as thin as broth. I was sleeping little then, waking early to read poetry, to journal, but I was unable to remain with paragraphs. Pages of text felt as overwhelming as the sight of Pete's sallow color and skeletal shape. The girls were not yet two and I had to keep them occupied and out of the way of the cleaning lady. She'd be in our house for four or five hours—running the vacuum, pushing a mop and hoisting a bucket upstairs. But after she left, I'd discover wads of dust beneath our bed, sauce still stuck on the range. Footprints clouded the floor like ghosted remains she failed to erase.

During those mornings, while everyone else slept, I tried to find my way around the uncertainty of Pete's health. I huddled close to the silence. I wrote words I have yet to return to. I revised my résumé and began freelance writing. We saved everything we brought in, unsure what the future might hold. Spring arrived and gradually his face again held color, his pants hugged his waist. This house—our house—has witnessed all of it.

The girls are six now. So much of that time feels washed out, faded. Being together has become our cornerstone—our faith in one another paramount. After the dinner dishes are put away, we head onto the porch where the girls like to play the telephone game. We sit beside one another and one person whispers a sentence to the person beside her and the meaning changes with each listener. Weekends when Pete isn't working, we hike at a state park or pick apples at a local orchard. At night, after presetting the coffee pot and locking the back door, I creep into the girls' room, push their hair back, kiss their faces. I whisper that I love them. Hope the words take root, offer steadiness for whatever lies ahead.

# ONCE, SOMETHING BAD HAPPENED TO US

The hush from Pete's morning shower wakes me. Moonlight etches the space around the blinds. Pete just a steamy room away, and yet in the darkness distance feels greater.

When the girls were babies, I didn't think about what it meant to kiss him goodbye in the morning or greet him when we both reconnected after work. I thought the two of us would grow old together. I imagined us retired and living in the woods, wearing elastic-banded pants and sipping coffee, digging into plates of fried eggs, reading for hours, maybe taking our aching bones for a hike. Back then, time stretched out like a dog in a raft of sun unaware of anything else but that moment.

\* \* \*

It's September 27, 2010, and Pete hasn't been healthy for months. A few days ago, he accidentally touched his spleen and was shocked to discover it was as hard and large as a melon.

I am home with the girls today while Pete's at the oncologist his doctor referred him to. I imagine him stretched on his stomach, hugging the table. "This is going to pinch a bit," I imagine the oncologist saying. "You'll feel some pressure," but Pete isn't really aware of what's happening. He hears the dull hum of a lawn mower, a distant car horn, the beeping of a garbage truck as it reverses. Maybe he's looking out the window at traffic on Highway 52 speeding by as a nurse swabs his back. Unlike me, Pete isn't bracing himself. This is just what needs to be done.

Pete's suit jacket is folded over a chair; he's thinking about getting back to work. He's only been at his job for three weeks, and the rest of the boxes from Philadelphia have yet to be opened.

Maybe he already knew on some level. For months he'd been losing weight and felt wrung out with exhaustion. It took two or three alarms to get him up in the morning and he'd slump over, fall asleep in a chair or on the bare floor within minutes of arriving home.

The girls are just shy of two years old and when they insert the needle into Pete's back for the bone marrow biopsy, maybe he's thinking about them.

\* \* \*

"How is Pete?" the friends who know often ask. "He's in remission now, right?"

"There is no remission," I'll say. "Not with his type of leukemia."

An awkward silence ensues.

Chronic myelogenous leukemia or CML is caused by a defect that triggers white blood cells to increase. The chromosome is called the Philadelphia gene, and in patients with CML the Philadelphia chromosomes replace the cells that produce normal blood cells. No treatment can destroy all the leukemic cells, but it's progress can be slowed.

A normal range for a white blood count is 5,000 to 10,000. In the fall of 2010, Pete's white blood count was 345,000 and the first time they tested his blood they detected a defect in every one of his white blood cells. Pete's most recent test showed 0.0001 of the Philadelphia chromosome in his blood. It isn't remission because the leukemic cells are still present, but it's close.

* * *

As a child, I was obsessed with death. Not just what happened upon death, but the actual process of dying. On the weekends when my parents would be busy hanging laundry on the backyard clothesline or sweeping out the garage, I'd create a potion in a plastic cup using household cleaners Mom kept on the shelf near the wash machine. I mixed Tide with Spic n Span, sprinkled Ajax, Downey, Drano, a few glugs of vinegar, and a squirt of lemony furniture polish, and stirred. The window above the stationary tub was at the surface of our driveway and thick with cobwebs, so I could almost imagine that I was elsewhere—perhaps an inhabitant of my own land. I didn't turn on the overhead lights, but moved around the milky haze, motes of dust floating on beams of sunlight. In the basement chill, everything outside had a tunneled sound to it: Dad unspooling the hose, Michael whizzing by on his bike, the whap of my sister's jump rope as she sang a Girl Scout song about "bringing home her baby bumblebee" over and over again.

As I turned the chunky concoction, my gangly legs and other shortcomings faded. With each stir, I could feel my hopes rising. Once smooth, it was ready. Armed with Q-tips I'd stuffed in the pockets of my shorts, I went onto our back patio, got onto my knees and dabbed the mixture on the ants that lived between the crevices of the bricks.

What if I figured out how we died? The reminders to look both ways on our bikes, to say our prayers and tie our shoes—would disappear. They'd print my name and photo in the newspaper and later include me in the history books.

Me.

"What are you doing?" Mom called as she clipped a pair of jeans on the line.

"Nothing."

"Well, you're going to wash that off the patio when you're through."

"I will," I promised.

The ants writhed back and forth in the blue broth; their movements dulled, eventually their individual carapaces no longer visible, just the fleck of an eyelash in a blue puddle.

As their movements slowed, I waited for something to happen— some sort of illumination. One moment these ants were alive, building their houses and carrying crumbs on their backs—now they were nothing. As I crouched over the splattered mess, I did not feel bad for killing them. The ants were so small, so inconsequential. I frequently used my pogo stick to pop their heads. I thought only of my own curiosity, attempted to satisfy this great uncertainty, believed it wholly within my powers.

I did not discover a great cure, but this little girl and her hopes to save all are still inside me. And when I find Pete asleep in a chair, book tented across his stomach, my breath catches. I take in his color, scan his body. The fear is always there.

\* \* \*

The November day we brought our daughters home from the hospital, I was petrified of hurting them. Eva was six pounds, Jolie four, and the newborn clothes they wore draped over their knuckles and gaped at their necks. We rolled hand towels around their heads and nestled them along their sides to make their car seats snug. Pete drove 15 miles per hour in a 40-mph speed zone. Once we arrived home, the dangers only quadrupled. We lived in a two-story brick colonial that looked and felt like a saltbox. One time while putting in a toilet paper dispenser, Pete reached his hand between the drywall to show me the insulation: newspaper ads from 1942.

Our house was far from warm, so we dialed up the heat and hoped for the best, dressing the girls in undershirts and thick stretch pants, knit hats.

We set a bassinette in our room, only the sounds of their breathing were too new. I didn't know when a sigh would become a cry or if a gurgled sound was actually someone choking. I tried to calm my fears by bringing one of the girls into our bed where I could keep watch over her, but as soon as I felt myself on the verge of falling asleep, I'd jolt awake, terrified that I'd roll over and crush her. After a week, we moved them into their own room, the heads of their cribs meeting in a backward L. At some point the shuttling in and out, the thin cage of their chests—every sound and movement became familiar.

\* \* \*

Now his hair is mostly gone. Not from the chemotherapy or Tasigna, the medication he takes every day for his leukemia, but from life. Recently I woke in the middle of the night to find him sitting upright in the dark, neck crooked on the headboard. "Are you okay?" I asked. "What's wrong?"

Pete tells me that earlier that day he'd gotten a raspberry seed caught between his teeth and while he'd flossed the seed away, the pain had continued. This happens more and more lately. His back hurts all the time. When Pete went for a run last month, he returned home limping. He is not alone. This winter I was yet again diagnosed with a stress fracture. And yet there was a time I didn't know if such instances would be available to us.

In the beginning I didn't question any of it.

\* \* \*

On our second date, Pete came to visit me for the weekend in Altoona, Pennsylvania, where I was teaching writing and working on my first book, a collection of short stories. I'd invited another faculty member and his family to join us for dinner and had made my mom's lasagna, laden with spinach and mozzarella. Six o'clock came and went, then

seven. No Pete. My friends' daughter had finished most of the crackers I'd set out and the lasagna—warming in the oven, was getting dry.
We'd long since opened the wine and ate quickly.

"We're so sorry we didn't get to meet Pete," they said at the door,
holding their daughter in their arms and giving me quick hugs. Pete
didn't have a cell phone and when his older Blazer trundled up the
drive it was so late that I momentarily froze in fear.

He was even skinnier than I recalled, but there was a familiarity
to his embrace, as if it wasn't until we were together that I realized
what I'd been missing. He sat down and ate three enormous slices
of lasagna, speaking little between bites, nodding his head as if he
were having a conversation with his dinner. He brought a six-pack
and after he washed the dishes, we moved to the couch and opened
our beers. Here it was fall and my position at the university ended
at the conclusion of the semester. I felt exceedingly more pressure to
publish my work so I could secure a tenure-track job. Pete listened,
and I found the clench I'd been carrying around all week eased. He
took my hand, then shook it as he talked so each word had its own
beat. "I've never spoken with someone like this before," he said. "It's
never been so easy."

* * *

That October, during those first blurry weeks of his diagnosis,
we arranged for a river birch to be planted in our backyard. We'd
placed one outside our home in Evergreen Park, and over time the
girth of the trunks quadrupled, the bark as ruffled as fresh pencil
shavings. Unlike our previous home, this one was newly built with
ample insulation and hardwood floors, windows that didn't require
us to cover them with plastic in winter. It seemed our real life was
beginning.

The girls were down for their naps; the sun was high, the sky
as blue as a drugstore postcard. I watched the landscaper back his

pickup onto the drive, sapling tipped over the truck bed, leaves and branches stretched over the cab, nearly obstructing the windshield.

Another pickup parked at the curb and three tanned men got out, grabbed a wheelbarrow from the back, and heaved the sapling into it. One man dug a hole, his shovel scraped and pitched the rocky soil; muscles plateaued on his back, his skin as smooth as peanut butter. At that point Pete had lost so much weight that the excess leather of his belt hung from him like an extra appendage. I bought him jeans with a thirty-inch waist and they still bagged his midsection. When he got undressed at night, I turned away.

As the hole deepened, the graveled sound grew muffled and soon the man jumped inside the hole and continued digging from inside, the shovel visible for a moment each time he heaved a fan of dirt overhead. When they finally lowered the tree into the hole, it looked so spindly I doubted it would survive the year.

After the men left, I stood alone with the landscaper in the grass, his suntanned face and white brush of hair. He wore a T-shirt with a company logo tucked into cargo shorts, hiking boots. He instructed me to soak the ground surrounding the tree during the start and end of the day for the next three months and then I'd need to pound fertilizer spikes into the dirt around the base twice a year. Something about his attire, the deliberateness of his words, the love he had for this young tree—and my eyes welled up. I thought of this—putting spikes in the ground months from now and the idea of that time socked me. I had no notion of what my life would be like then and considering the future felt like an insult.

"You'll want to space them out," he said, and I began to cry.

"My husband has cancer," I said. "We just found out."

The sun beat down on us, the leaves of the new tree limp, the sky a forever blue and cloudless. "I'm sorry, ma'am," he said. I nodded, wiped my face, and took a few steps back. No one had ever called me ma'am. I was no longer a child. I was the adult.

* * *

I've tried to write about Pete's illness many different ways: a straight chronological narrative, a series of letters to each girl during which time I finally told them of his diagnosis. There are a few poems as well. I thought that piece would be the most powerful thing I'd ever write, as if nothing in the past or present could match the natural arc of our lives at that time: the inciting incident, the crisis, the falling action. But I could never figure out what I wanted to say. Once, something bad happened to us. Despite the fact that we are good people, Pete has cancer. Lots of people get sick and die.

"What's important about this story?" An editor once asked. I didn't have an answer. Maybe I never will.

* * *

While we waited for the oral chemotherapy to kick in, for his appetite to return, and for him to make it through the evening without falling asleep before dinner, we did normal everyday things. He went to his office. I hired a babysitter so I could take my laptop to the local coffee shop and write. One weekend we outfitted the girls in swim diapers and took them to an indoor water park where Pete went down a slide with one of the girls on his lap and upon the impact of the water, she had what was henceforth known as a "poo-nami." All of us quickly exited the pool, the offending girl and her diaper held an arm's length away. It quickly became a family joke and poo-nami was used to describe any catastrophic event with poop.

We were like any other family except that we had this great secret. We live in a small town and Pete didn't want to be known as the guy with cancer. Other than our families and my best friends, we didn't tell anyone. If they didn't know about the cancer, maybe it wasn't real.

* * *

I want to say that I don't take a moment for granted. I want to say that I don't raise my voice when Pete angers me like last year when a sex offender moved down our street and I'd wake in the morning to discover that Pete had gone to bed after me and left the door unlocked.

I want you to think I'm no longer afraid of death. But that wouldn't be true.

\* \* \*

Around this time, other men fascinated me. I'd stare at their complexions, the solidity of their backs and shoulders, their full heads of hair. I imagined the blood in their bodies flowing unencumbered by an excess of white blood cells. When Brad, a male friend I hadn't heard from in years, called, the heft of our secret prodded the back of my throat. The girls were playing in the basement and I paced back and forth in the kitchen, looked out the window at the river birch as we talked. I wanted to tell him the truth when he asked how I was. He was still single at the time and while we'd never dated, the possibility had always existed and now, as we spoke, I imagined a whole different reality: If Pete died, I'd take up with Brad. There would be no white pillboxes and when he nodded off, I wouldn't draw close to hear the pulse of his breath. After thinking about Brad and this imagined narrative, my own thoughts sickening me, at day's end, I greeted Pete with a long hug. I silently vowed not to go there again.

\* \* \*

We saved every cent. We held onto the Craigslist couch, my ten-year-old Subaru, the wobbly table from my graduate school days. Still, in the months following Pete's diagnosis, I woke at 4:30 a.m., unable to sleep. I journaled in the dark quiet while everyone was asleep and familiarized myself with our new reality. I sat at the kitchen table with a mug of coffee and a book of poems. Long a lover of short stories, I had begun to read poetry. Something about the white space and heft of each word felt comforting and right. I'd begun an image journal and jotted down words that felt evocative—whittle, throb, root shadow, and the richness of those very words, copying them into a wire-bound notebook, offered solace. The act of living each day, hope.

\* \* \*

Eight months after his diagnosis we vacationed in Michigan, rented a two-bedroom cabin a short walk to the lake. I packed sand toys and snacks and two inflatable rafts. I coated the girls in sunscreen and offered juice boxes. Pete and I took turns holding the girls' hands as we stood at the water's edge. The girls squealed each time the water eclipsed their toes. The sun hot. Pete dug in the sand with a plastic shovel, filled a bucket with water and then dumped it in the moat he hollowed out. The girls looked as if they'd rolled in cinnamon and sugar. I stood them up, cupped my hands with water and spread this over their arms and legs, and then hoisted them into the rafts. They were tiny things with three inflatable donuts, a yellow rope for tugging. Pete and I pulled the girls in circles. The waves rocked the floats, the water warm. The jostling reminded me of how the girls once existed inside me, how my pregnancy was considered high-risk and each week I surrendered to ultrasound. The technician would paint my belly with sticky gel and I'd sit back with a towel draped over my underwear and marvel at the flickering picture projected on the screen—this part of my insides illuminated. I memorized their fully shaped limbs, the shady contours of organs inside two separate sacs of fluid. The technician would move the wand and click the buttons on her computer, measure the size of femur and cranium and these measurements were then used to determine if the girls were healthy and growing.

The thermometer edged past 90 degrees and the girls needed to get out of the sun and down for a nap. Pete handed me the rope to his raft, lifted his arms overhead and dove. A trail of bubbles appeared in his wake. After several seconds, he popped his head up, broke the surface. He grinned several feet in the distance. His face and shaven head slick with water. How did it feel to leave us for those few moments? He squinted. Water dribbled his nose. He rubbed his face. "The water's great," he said. "Your turn."

# THE PERILS OF GIRLHOOD

The bodies of Liberty German and Abigail Williams were found in a wooded area about fifty feet north of Deer Creek in Delphi, Indiana. They weren't far from the Old Monon Trail, where Liberty's older sister dropped off the middle schoolers to go hiking on an unseasonably warm day on February 13, 2017.

Liberty excelled in math and science. In all the newspaper photos the eighth grader's broad face grinned wide with confidence. Her corn-silk colored hair hung in loose waves, maybe unbrushed, or maybe just indifferent. Liberty was also the one who carried a cell phone with her that day. She loved softball and that year Abigail had promised to join Liberty's team.

At thirteen, Abigail was a year younger. In the photo printed in the newspaper, she wore a sundress with an oversized sun hat. A two-inch band of fabric at the crown matched her dress. Her front teeth were nubs, not yet fully grown. Everything I learned about them came from newspaper articles I read and reread.

That was four years ago, when my twin daughters were eight and years away from being teenagers. Now they are twelve, just one year younger than Abigail, and I have become a crucible of fear. When a TV show featured a special on Liberty and Abigail in April 2020, I didn't let the girls watch it. But I did. Riveted by the screen, I tried to make sense of the murders.

We live twenty miles from Delphi, in West Lafayette, Indiana. We moved here in 2010 after living in Philadelphia while my husband finished school and I worked as a freelance writer. In between time at my desk, I took care of our girls. In the mornings I pushed them in a double stroller to Fairmont Park, which we nicknamed Tree Park because it was hidden beneath a towering mass of craggy oaks. During afternoon strolls we bumped along cobblestone streets southeast of our apartment past million-dollar flats to Schuylkill Park. There were only two baby swings, so I placed the girls in one swing, back-to-back, like some chubby two-sided mammal. Then, in December, at thirteen months old, Eva had her first seizure.

Despite subsequent testing, the doctors never could provide a reason for Eva's initial life-threatening seizure, one that left her intubated, a respirator tunneling up and down, breathing for her. All of this alerted me to my daughter's mortality.

One of the reasons we moved to Indiana was because we thought it would be a safe place to raise our girls. For a while it was. They were eight when Liberty and Abigail were murdered.

\* \* \*

I've read numerous articles about the murders, searching for some shred of evidence, some hidden rationale for this crime, but the more I read, the faster the details fade, like water smearing ink on a handwritten letter. The girls were hiking alone on a day off school. Liberty was actively posting on Snapchat as they walked. I imagine them goofing around, teasing each other about crushes, asking if they like the latest song by Dua Lipa, maybe singing a few lines at the top of their lungs. I see them on the bridge and then I see myself walking with my own best friend from junior high. Thirty years earlier and it could have been me or my classmates. It could still be my daughters, their friends.

I've shared these concerns with my husband. What if the murderer is living in our midst? How could we keep our daughters safe? He looked at me, my arms full of a stack of folded clothes, then gently said that we couldn't live that way. And I thought: but we will, we do. All women at some point fear.

Images of my own daughters blanket our refrigerator. In the girls' preschool photo, they wear matching corduroy dresses and hold hands. Jolie wears a headband that highlights her apple-shaped face. Eva's lips are pursed together like a walnut as she blows a channel of air at an unforeseen yellow duckie. Meanwhile, the school photographer stands behind her camera and squeezes the toy as she prepares the shot. "Blow on the duckie," she says to the girls, and my daughters, obedient as ever, comply.

One day soon after the murders, the girls were with me as I exited the grocery store when a pickup truck with wheel wells taller than their heads jerked forward and nearly hit Eva. I grabbed her by the shoulders and yanked her close to me. "That truck could have hit you!" I yelled. The truck had passed, so I turned around, pointed. "What would happen if you were hit?"

"I'd get run over," Eva said.

"You'd be crushed!" I announced, wanting her fear to match or exceed my own.

The truck grumbled away, its gruff sounds gradually fading.

"When we leave the house or car, you should not be looking at your shoes," I said. "You should be taking stock of what's going on around you."

"What's 'taking stock' mean?" asked Jolie, turning her head like some wind-up toy.

"It means 'taking note of. Noticing.' Does that make sense?"

"Uh-huh," the girls said.

I pushed the grocery cart to the car and opened the trunk. The girls darted for their doors.

Groceries in cloth bags. A peerless sky. Birds twittered overhead as the giant flag at the front of the grocery store flapped. Somewhere in Delphi two women sat waiting for the murderer of their daughters to be brought to justice. Their eyes were blurry and headachy and in this way time passed. Maybe one spooled yarn to keep her fingers busy. The other could be tapping a fingernail against an empty can of soda. Another day.

My daughters slammed their car doors. I heaved the bags into the trunk. Already they had begun to fight over whose turn it was to read the same book they'd been reading all summer. It's a graphic novel about a girl with embarrassing braces and an awkward existence. "It's my turn," said Eva. "You read it before."

"But I didn't finish it," said Jolie. I glanced at them in the rearview mirror yanking the paperback between them.

As they argued, everything inside me stiffened; I centered on the chirpy sound of their voices, brilliantly alive.

\* \* \*

I remember my daughters in denim overalls with snaps inside the "U" of their legs, hand-me-down floral Gap raincoats from their cousins, pink snowsuits and knit gloves on strings that looped the arms of their jackets. We were told that it was dangerous to put them to sleep with blankets or pillows, so during the girls' first two winters we put them in cotton sleepers and then zipped them into second fleeces.

They ate sitting upright in high chairs: Cheerios and toast cut into one-inch strips, yogurt and scrambled eggs. I inserted chunks of melon into a mesh contraption so the girls could hold the fruit like a Popsicle and gum it without choking. But after Eva's initial hospitalization and subsequent seizures, I remained on edge, and every potential harm could ignite fear in me like flammable gas.

During that year in Philadelphia, the girls woke early and after breakfast I popped them in the stroller. We headed to Tree Park.

Just off the Ben Franklin Parkway, and east of the narrow steps of the Philadelphia Museum of Art with its bronze sculpture of a triumphant Rocky Balboa, morning traffic crawled alongside us. As I pushed the stroller, I watched the perimeter where the girls had been known to toss their shoes. There was a small translucent square of vinyl on the top of the stroller and I could just make out the bowls of their heads.

On one early morning jaunt, I turned the stroller into the park, pushed it over the cracked sidewalk with its exposed tree roots, and discovered three men fast asleep beneath the play structure. They were nestled inside sleeping bags, heads pillowed on backpacks and duffels. Their hair was matted and disheveled, the nylon of their sleeping bags sooty. I paused.

Something about their sleeping shapes made them familiar, as if we were personally acquainted, and I felt as if the longer we remained, the greater likelihood that the same misfortune might befall us. I know it makes no sense, but who is to say what, if anything, draws trouble? Would any mother be willing to gamble her child's future well-being?

I've read that a woman's brain actually changes with motherhood. In the maternal brain, the amygdala, which manages memories and fear reactions, is strengthened in the weeks and months after childbirth. Coupled with hormones, some of the new neural pathways that develop are dedicated to vigilance and survival. It's nearly impossible to communicate the fears we hold for our children or the way our minds react to those fears. Few crimes are committed by unknown perpetrators, yet this part of my brain with its well-worn track of fears is far from rational. All I ever wanted was to feel safe and protect the ones I love from harm.

I backed up the stroller, and turned in the direction we came. I sped home. Somewhere these men had families—mothers who once woke to feed them in the middle of the night and rock them back to sleep. But now they lived here—wandered the city's streets and playgrounds, made beds on mulch and leaves. All day I continued to think of those sleeping men. I wondered if their mothers knew where they were, felt the void of their absence.

\* \* \*

One morning in my childhood home, as I poured milk over my cornflakes, I saw his face on the side of the carton. It was 1984 when the National Child Safety Council began its Missing Children Milk Carton Program, and I assumed the boy staring back at me was Adam Walsh. They'd announced on the news that he was missing, only this boy was the same age as me with straggly hair and bangs. It said he had blue eyes and was from New York and if you saw him, to call the 1-800 number.

Mom sliced bananas over my cereal, but her voice, her presence seemed far away, and for a moment I was Adam Walsh, locked away in a damp, dark place with only the memory of my parents, my bedroom, the breakfasts we shared around the kitchen table. I scooped cereal into my mouth and chewed harder as if the great churning could fix me forever in our sun-bleached kitchen.

In the 1980s, stranger danger was a real thing, prompted by the abduction of Adam Walsh, who in July 1981 had been shopping with his mother at a Florida mall when she left him alongside several other boys playing an Atari game. She was gone for less than ten minutes. His abduction set the nation on high alert. Children like me were told to stick together and to be watchful for strangers. "Somewhere along the way, we allowed fear to get inside us," says Paul Crenshaw in *Salon*. "Stranger danger made us fear strangers, so we began to see everyone as dangerous."

Later that month, our teacher led our class to the gym and instructed us to line up in front of a long table. Police officers stood on one side with boxes of index cards and ink. The officer asked my name, printed it in large block letters on the top of a card, then he had me stretch out my hand. He pressed each finger on a small pad of ink, rolled it side to side, then did the same thing on the card, transferring the print. He did this with each of my blackened fingers and then put the card aside to dry. I wiped my fingers and stared at my card in its place on the table. Now, if someone took me, maybe I'd be easier to find.

\* \* \*

Two weeks after the murders in Delphi, there was a new development. The Carroll County sheriff released an audio recording of the assailant found on Liberty German's cell phone. "Down the river," said the recording. "Down the river. Down the river. Down the river," it said, and coupled with the grainy photo of a heavy-set man in a navy windbreaker, there was the sense that resolution was imminent.

In the morning, I whisked the newspaper from the lawn while still in my pajamas. I thought it possible to shelter our girls by learning everything I could about the fate of Liberty and Abigail. I began to play the recording two and three times a day. The phone was discovered half a mile down the bank of Deer Creek near the Monon High Bridge, the train trestle bridge where the girls were last spotted.

I wondered about Liberty. Hailed a hero for turning on her phone's audio, she took two photographs that afternoon and posted them on Snapchat. The first was at 2:07 p.m. of Abigail, striking a pose on the bridge. In the distance, you can see a man approaching. The second photo was of the man with his hands in the pockets of his jeans. At what point did a weird, unsettled feeling shift to out-and-out terror? When did their innocent hike during a day off school become a failed sprint for survival? And then, what happened next?

By 3:30 p.m. the girls weren't answering their phones.

Moments of terror happen fast.

The night of Eva's first seizure, I had been at the store. When I entered our Philadelphia apartment, a sack of groceries on my shoulder, Pete stood in our kitchen like a man before a firing squad. He held Eva sideways in his arms. "Why isn't she in her bed?" I asked. He held Eva as if she were made of glass, her head in the bend of his left elbow, her legs poking his right.

A cold whip of fear shot through me.

"What's wrong?"

She wore a green fuzzy sleeper with a bear on the chest. Her tiny arms and legs were going *jerk jerk jerk* while her neck remained stuck in a one-two beat.

"What's happening? What happened?"

Her eyes were slitted open but unseeing, the pupils sailing back and forth. The skin on her face had whitened, the lips a faint shade of blue. I called 911, and as I placed the phone to my ear, my husband leaned over Eva, placed his mouth over hers, and breathed.

After Pete left with Eva to meet the ambulance, I ran down the hall, knocked on doors, begging someone to answer. My feet slip slopped on the waxed floors past fake ferns, my fists pounding on every door as sirens screamed down the street. Jolie was still asleep in her crib and I needed someone to stay with her. Help! Please help! I begged.

No one answered.

I returned to the apartment and once I saw that Jolie was fine, I paced the floors. A wall of windows lined one wall of the apartment and tall buildings burnished the night with boxes of light. Beyond were nameless people enjoying their dinners, laughing and chatting, breathing without worry.

I balled my fists and began to cry.

If the ER had not been a seven-minute ambulance ride away, if the attending physician had not been able to intubate Eva—two other doctors that night had been unsuccessful—I might be another mother, one of the ones I imagine in Delphi, gazing out the window at nothing in particular. I cannot help but imagine how different the world looks to these women now: the blank spaces in the trees shred the light; remaining leaves curled up like an old man's arthritic hand while others skitter along the sidewalk. The fear and hope intermingling.

* * *

At twelve, my daughters made plans with friends away from home. They liked to go to Happy Hollow Park; a nature area nestled in the woods about a half mile from our home. The park has several picnic shelters and two large climbing structures with a twisty slide, monkey bars, and half a dozen swings. Hidden behind feathery green leaves, two miles of paved hiking trails surrounded the park. A creek bisects all of this, the constant woosh a backdrop to children's play.

While they were no longer interested in scrambling up the climbing wall or playing hide-and-seek, they spent hours on a rope swing someone had hung from one of the ancient trees. They went with Violet, a neighbor girl who is the same age as them, and each time before they left, I told them to stay together.

"We will," they sang.

It was a Saturday in late fall, the sun milky white when the three of them skipped away for the swing. While they were gone, I might have read the paper or answered an email, or done something else without consequence. What I do know is that I was home when Eva fled in the back door with a red nose and gummy eyes.

"What's wrong?" I asked. "Where's your sister?" Panic tore through me and I shot up from my seat as if I'd been struck with a diviner rod and it had touched a truth that had been there all along.

She wiped her face.

"What happened?" I asked. The drum of my own heartbeat filled my ears.

Eva began to cry harder.

"Okay," I told her, placing an arm around her shoulders. "It's okay," and I led her to a kitchen chair. Even though she was too old, I pulled her onto my lap. Her weight settled on me. She fiddled with her hands.

"There was a man. He was watching us."

"A man?" I asked, while pushing her up. "Let's go. Show me."

We jogged down our block and when we turned onto the next street, we spied Jolie and Violet walking toward us. It wasn't until we stopped that I realized that I had lost sensation in the lower half of my body. "Are you all right? What happened?" my legs buzzed and my words couldn't form fast enough.

Jolie and Violet looked at each other. Shrugged.

"What about the man?" I asked.

Jolie screwed up her mouth like she'd bitten something sour. "We didn't see him," and shrugged. This struck me as odd.

I talked the girls into following me back to the swing. They stood on the hiking path practicing pirouettes as I climbed over the split wood fence that bordered the path, and then headed down the hill to the swing. I circled the area, kicked at the brush, unsure of what I was looking for. There was no one there. The girls turned and ran ahead of me, headed back home. I took my time.

Sometimes the fear feels like a river roiling through my chest. Other times it's like a smoldering fire that when fanned, erupts into a blaze. I practice acknowledging these feelings so that they do not take me hostage. But no amount of practice prepares you for when the fire, in a gust of wind, catches on, and engulfs an entire forest.

\* \* \*

In 2017, investigators released a sketch of a man they believed to be a possible suspect in the Liberty and Abigail case, but they updated it in 2019 to reflect additional witness accounts. This recent sketch makes the man look much younger than the initial image. Police say the suspect is between the ages of eighteen and forty, a white male with reddish brown hair who is "hiding in plain sight."

During the episode that aired in April 2020 of *In Pursuit with John Walsh*, Walsh and his son Callahan asked viewers to call in to the show with anonymous tips and leads in "an attempt to bring a killer to justice." John Walsh's own son, Adam Walsh, was murdered in 1981. He had been the boy from the shopping mall, perhaps the reason the police department fingerprinted my classmates and me. Anti-crime activism became the elder Walsh's life work. A few days after his son's funeral, Walsh's parents started the Adam Walsh Outreach Center for Missing Children, and in 1988 he began hosting *America's Most Wanted*.

Callahan Walsh made a trip to Delphi to examine video evidence, audio, and the two sketches from possible witnesses. After talking with the Carroll County sheriff, Callahan Walsh walked the narrow rickety bridge where Liberty's photos were taken, the creek below a rush of brown silt. Callahan Walsh said he believed the killer was someone who grew up in Delphi and knew the area well. He believes the murderer is someone who knows the trails "like the back of his hand."

Despite the tips received once the show aired, the new sketch, the audio recording, and the recent arrest of an accused, the murder of Liberty and Abigail may never be solved. One thing remains clear: something frightened Liberty, put her on edge enough for her to turn on her phone's recording device. And maybe this is what I find more unsettling than the fact that a murderer walks free. In their final moments, these two girls were scared. Frightened to a degree that they most likely had never before experienced, and they only had trees as witnesses.

* * *

Sometimes I'll look at the photos of my daughters on the refrigerator and I'll be shocked by how much they've changed. Eva's features are more defined. She tilts her head when she laughs, as if she's trying to tip out every crumb of joy. Jolie's face has thinned, her gaze direct. When she talks there is the sense that each word exists for her purpose alone.

And then I play a little game. I glance at the earliest image of them—ten months old with round faces and chunked fists in Philadelphia—and then I look at the photo that follows this chronologically all the way to the most recent images from fifth grade. I try to glimpse the people they will become, as if by imagining their future, I can guarantee they'll have one.

# LOCK ME!

I am not afraid of crocodiles. Whenever I'd seen crocodiles they were held captive behind glass or at a safe distance. It would be irrational to be frightened by something that lives so far from my home. Black vultures, anacondas, jaguars, and other carnivores prey on Orinoco crocodiles. Normally docile, female crocodiles can become aggressive while nesting.

\* \* \*

My neighbor begins the group text. She sends a screenshot of a map of the sexual predators who live in our neighborhood. I didn't even know such a site existed. I'm driving more than seventy miles to Indianapolis twice a week to teach creative writing as an adjunct. There is a pile of laundry that may never be folded, and my daughters are fighting. I stop putting away the dinner leftovers and scroll the screen. The map is lilac. Tiny yellow cones mark where predators reside. A friend's message guts me: *The guy in the blue house, three down from you, is on the list.*

\* \* \*

Alan Lee Litman's earliest creations were far from successes. He invented his waterless egg cooker in his basement laboratory in 1963. He'd also placed his hopes on an infrared nursing bottle heater, but then a young female teacher from the high school where his wife taught was mugged. Litman and his wife, Doris, began to discuss products a woman might use to protect herself.

\* \* \*

The first few days after my neighbor's text, I meet my daughters at their bus stop. I don't want to overreact, but here I am. Normally they walk home alone. They don't question my presence.

I realize these anxieties are likely irrational. And yet there they are, holding me prisoner. We live in a small town several miles from Indianapolis and I am a white woman. Other women have not benefited from the safety of these advantages. And yet my fears have put me on a path, real or imagined, that is difficult to sidestep.

\* \* \*

The dreams begin my sophomore year of college. They are all the same. I am walking alone when someone grabs me from behind, smothers a hand across my mouth, and drags me into a dark alley. What happens next is less clear but there are always hands groping, holding me. Try as I might, I am unable to break free.

\* \* \*

Alan Litman experimented with kerosene, Freon, and sulfuric acid—chemicals that act as severe irritants and could be sprayed into eyes and faces. He ultimately chose chloroacetophenone, a chemical the U.S. military used as a tear gas during World War II to create his "Chemical Mace." Since it was already a known irritant, he did not receive a patent.

\* \* \*

"Which one do you want?" asked Dad, pointing to the display of Mace near the cash register. After I told him about the feeling that I would soon be harmed, he took me to a gun shop during a weekend visit home from college. The store looked like any other gun shop I'd visited with him. The aisles were low and stocked with ammunition and cleaning supplies. Gun cases and rifle holsters hung from racks; the floors wrecked linoleum. A glass case lined the length of the wall. Inside, handguns splayed shelves like bones. There were pink canisters of Mace that fit perfectly in your hand and camouflage ones that I assumed were used while hunting in the woods. I pretended to look through the different varieties and checked in with my fear. It followed me everywhere.

* * *

During the dry season, female crocodiles retreat to riverbanks where they dig holes in the sand and lay forty to sixty eggs. The incubation temperature during the first few weeks determines the sex of their offspring. Warmer temperatures produce males.

* * *

I secure a sticky note above the knob of our back door with tape that says *Lock Me!* The paper is magenta, my words printed in permanent marker. Still, my husband, who works late hours, often fails to lock the door. When I wake, stumble bleary-eyed toward the coffee pot and see that the door has remained unlocked all night, I feel a rush of fright and fury. I lift the kitchen shade an inch and peer at the park. I can see the two picnic benches where I sat with the girls the day we moved to Indiana. The girls had awoken just as we pulled into our new driveway. I offered them bowls of Goldfish crackers and sippy cups of juice. They were dazed from their naps, but stared at the two swings, the play structure that looks like a castle, a mini surfboard on springs. Back then I had imagined games of hide-and-seek with neighborhood playmates, hours spent swinging, popsicles on the porch. Now I'm not even sure if I should let them go to the park alone. When they do go, I stand at this window. I imagine him lumbering up the sidewalk, lurking beneath the ancient oak, a hand fingering the callused bark, and then I see myself speeding out the back door, chest heaving, blood rushing, standing in front of him waving an outstretched finger like a poker that's been roasting in hot coals for days.

\* \* \*

It is well-documented that women experience more fear and anxiety than men. Some of this stems from the fact women are exposed to more traumatic events such as rape, attempted rape, and abuse, closely tied to PTSD and other anxiety disorders.

\* \* \*

Litman received a patent in 1969 for the spray bottle he invented to hold the pocket-sized Mace. He then opened the General Ordnance Equipment Corporation, a business that created nonlethal weapons like Pepper Fog, a tear smoke detonator and an aerosol container of tear gas called the Chemical Baton.

\* \* \*

I lived in Daum, one of the older dormitories at the University of Iowa. The windows were tall and dusty, white paint layered the walls; they repurposed the old cafeteria with its spindle-backed chairs and tables into a study room. Shelves where dirty food trays once stacked stood empty, and I'd think of the women who lived there when the dorm first opened in the 1960s. Girls the same age as I was but they wore dresses and stockings, hair set in rollers each night. There was an eerie emptiness to the place, like all the women who lived there left an echo of their younger selves, a strangled sound that seeped from the cobwebbed ceiling.

\* \* \*

The Tippecanoe County Sheriff's Office website says he is five feet nine, 132 pounds, with brown hair and brown eyes. He has been in and out of prison since he was eighteen and was first charged with child molestation. I enlarge the picture of his face, peer at the screen in my hand. He has long wavy hair and a heavy beard that laps his chin. It looks scruffy. He looks *scruffy*, the same name one of my twin daughters gave to the oversized stuffed puppy she cuddles with in bed. That night I make sure the doors are locked and implore Pete to do the same. In bed, I remain awake, wondering what the predator did and to whom.

* * *

In one video a female crocodile lurks in murky water along the sandy bank where her eggs are buried. Six conservationists and handlers brace long wooden rods. When one of the conservationists uses his hands to dig for her eggs, the crocodile thrashes her tail and throws herself up on the bank, snapping her jaws. The other handlers wave their rods in front of her. "I've found them," the conservationist says, pointing to the creamy speckled shells they will take to a government-run ranch. The men wave their sticks and she retreats into the water where she watches them with yellow-green eyes.

* * *

I can still recall the feel of it in my hand walking home from the campus library. It would be late and the streets absent of cars. Thumping music traveled from downtown bars as if through a tunnel. I buried my hands in the pockets of my barn jacket and my right hand held the Mace. The canister was black and a flip-top safety cap comprised the cover. Below this was a red pad that when pressed ejected the spray. I memorized the feel of this red button, moved my thumb back and forth across its four raised lines.

\* \* \*

I hire a babysitter for the days I teach. My daughters do not like her. She is a college student with a look as blank as a sheaf of paper. When I tell the sitter there is a child molester down the street and ask her to keep the door locked, she says that she will. Yet each time I pull my car into the garage and step over the dog leash choking the stairs, I find the door unlocked.

\* \* \*

According to the CDC, exposure to chloroacetophenone irritates skin, can constrict airways, and causes fluid buildup in the lungs. Persistent contact with the eyes can cause corneal opacity and even blindness.

\* \* \*

Within hours of birth, baby crocodiles must find water or they will die. Once hatched, the mother crocodile scoops the wriggling babies into her open mouth and brings them to a protected pool. She can carry as many as fifteen babies in her mouth at once. When she opens her jaw the young scramble out like spring-operated toys.

\* \* \*

I finally see him on an unseasonably warm day in spring bent over a rectangular grill. The grill is a rusty green box and stands just a few inches off his front stoop. It is so small that he must crouch on the balls of his feet in front of it. Blue smoke funnels up. I can't smell the food. I'm too fixated on him. He's shirtless and wears cut-off black sweatpants; hair drips past his shoulders. Air in my lungs constricts and it feels like I am being held underwater. If I were closer I might see his tattoos: the Batman and Robin on his right arm, the Batmobile with the words *Pow!* and *Bam!*, the Chicken Boba Fett on his left thigh. But his back is to me and I hesitate to linger. I don't want him to realize that I have two daughters and that they live a few hundred feet from him. Now there is no denying it. He is real.

\* \* \*

My daughters still play dolls, only now they do so secretly, draping a sheet over chair backs and tucking themselves beneath. They prefer the rag dolls they've had since they were five with their soft cotton skin and yarn hair, lips a painted red bow. They sit on bent knees and tug on ill-fitting sweaters and tunics that catch on their dolls' lumpy heads. Then they stand their dolls upright, make them walk a few steps before placing them on their laps and undressing them. I never hear them telling their dolls that they need to finish their milk before they can have another cookie or that they must look both ways before crossing the street. They simply go through the act of getting ready for a day that never comes.

\* \* \*

Pete tries to teach the girls self-defense. He tells them to try and grab him. "Go on," he says, grinning. One of my daughters charges and grabs his wrist; my husband opens the hand of the arm she has grabbed and twists out toward the thumb, breaking her grasp. "Nice!" he says. My daughter giggles, covering her mouth with her fingers. "You don't want to pull away if someone grabs you," he says. "They'll only hold tighter. You try." I watch Pete clap a hand on my daughter's wrist, his hand as still as a loaf of bread. She flings her arm out, freeing herself from his hold. We all cheer.

\* \* \*

Research shows that women overestimate the potential of danger in comparison to men, and frequently expect harm. This ability to foresee situations as threatening developed as women tried to safeguard their offspring. When presented with a perceived threat, neuroscientists believe we activate the amygdala, the same region in our brains set off by exposure to the actual thing. This is where emotional memories reside. That means the fear response can be activated even if you don't interact with the real thing.

\* \* \*

I imagine I'll see him at our back door, letting himself into our kitchen. Our dog is old and sleeps soundly and somehow he will know this. He'll tiptoe up the stairs and creep into my daughters' room with the pink gingham curtains, the twin beds, the bookcase crammed with stuffed animals and graphic novels. Between their beds is a small side table with a lamp, its shade decorated with butterflies. I'll see him standing over them. He'll finger one end of the girls' cotton blanket—

\* \* \*

When I was young my mother used to tell me that I had an overactive imagination.

\* \* \*

Doris and Alan Litman kept a pet Orinoco crocodile in their basement. They named it Ernst.

\* \* \*

It happened my junior year of college, second semester, and more than a year after my dad bought me the Mace. Kevin had dark brown hair, nearly black, and I remember white flecks of dandruff peppering his navy pillowcase. We had gone out for beer.

\* \* \*

In one picture of Ernst taken in the Litman's home in the 1970s, he reclines in some sort of tank with his mouth open, snout tipped up, white teeth like spikes. Doris steadies her hand beneath his gaping jaw and leans in. She appears to be saying something to Ernst and he appears to be listening.

\* \* \*

I know his name. I know his height. I know his previous address. I know the dates of his arrests for suspended driving and I know when he was convicted for failing to register as a sex offender. Maybe I know too much.

\* \* \*

Alan Litman went on to specialize in safety and self-defense. He received patents for a burglar alarm and an "antipersonnel grenade." But the thing that puzzles me is his transformation from basement inventor of domestic creations to "pocked-sized personal protection." Something about that young female colleague of Doris Litman's must have shaken him. Maybe he imagined his own wife mugged on the streets of downtown Pittsburgh. Maybe Litman climbed the steps out of his basement laboratory and into the bright lights of the kitchen, and over Doris's meatloaf and mashed potatoes, found he could not stop thinking about the woman who had been attacked. At night, while he brushed his teeth and in the morning as he sipped his coffee, he thought about the young teacher.

\* \* \*

The one time I needed the Mace, I didn't have it. Kevin and I had been fooling around. Kissing, groping, laughing, which is why I thought he was making a joke when he pinned me on my back, straddled me, and told me I couldn't leave his bedroom. We'd gone out a few times before this and I laughed, tried to roll over. "You can't go," he said. "You aren't leaving." I scanned his face. He wasn't smiling. "Let me go," I said. I twisted my torso back and forth, tried to break free. "You're staying here all night," he told me. He held me by the tops of my arms and leaned his weight against me, a choking heaviness that scissored my breath. Around the door crept a faint purple hue from the fish tank in the living room. I don't know what lived in the tank, but I remember the faint musty smell of cedar and urine, the hum of fluorescent bars, the canister of Mace in my dorm room.

# DEEPER THAN THE EYE CAN SEE

*Stacy has just been admitted to the psychiatric floor of a hospital,* texts Liz, my college roommate from more than twenty years ago. *Can u talk?*

I stop the freelance assignment I'm working on and pick up the phone. Liz explains what she knows.

Earlier that day Stacy called Mara, a mutual friend of ours—Stacy was crying so hard she could barely get out the words to ask if Mara could watch her kids. As Liz says this, everything comes into focus. I'm standing in our office next to the printer. There are stacks of folders, a jar of pens. Beside this is a framed picture Pete gifted me one Mother's Day. In it, the girls are five and wear sundresses that tie behind their necks. I hold their hands, my elbows cocked. Snapped from behind and mid-stride, in the photo, my legs make long shadowed streams against the white cotton of my skirt. From the back, I look both powerful and unafraid, a woman launching into the future.

Why do you want me to watch the kids? Mara asked. Stacy could only sob. The rest of the story becomes murky. Mara takes Stacy to the hospital where, after a two-hour wait, the staff asks her a series of questions: How long have you been feeling this way? Do you want to hurt yourself? Do you have a plan?

"She planned to crash her car, only the kids were with her," says Liz.

The hospital did not have room to admit her, Liz reports, but Stacy's eighty-year-old mother drove her two hours west on I-80 to a small community hospital where they had beds available.

"Melissa, she had a f'ing plan," Liz had said. "A suicide plan." I had nodded, even though she couldn't see me. Inside I trembled.

I have had that kind of plan too.

Liz promises to call or text if she hears anything else. The call ends but I remain still. It seems like the least I can do.

\* \* \*

I received the message about Stacy just a few weeks into the news that Jolie's uveitis—an inflammation of the uvea—the middle portion of her eyes—had worsened. Left untreated it caused blindness. I cried for three days and had been finding my resolve when I learned about Stacy.

Hundreds of miles away, Stacy was on the verge of giving up, giving in. I had forgotten that even mothers have this choice.

Now I brush back Jolie's hair from her eyes before administering her morning drops of prednisolone, the first of four eye drops that will be evenly spaced throughout the day. I kiss her nose before handing her a Kleenex. She rubs her eyes, squints. "Ready?" I ask. On Fridays I hold a bag a frozen vegetables to her bicep, then inject my fourth grader with Humira; Saturday, after the four sets of drops, we administer cyclopentolate at bedtime, and this dilates her eyes. These drops burn and once Pete or I hold her steady and plink a drop of the medicine in her eye, she slaps hands to her face and then rocks back and forth.

"One more," I say, more for myself than to her.

In the fall of her kindergarten year, Jolie's knees swelled like softball helmets and walking became painful. She had no recollection of falling or bruising herself. An examination by a pediatric rheumatologist and subsequent blood work diagnosed her with juvenile idiopathic arthritis or JIA. Yet it wasn't until a routine eye exam three years later in March 2017 that she was diagnosed with uveitis, which is commonly associated with JIA. Until then, we had been able to control her flare-ups through NSAIDS and by applying packs of heat to her swelling joints. We quit gluten and dairy, and ate fish twice a week. But with the inflammation in her eyes, we were forced to inject her with methotrexate to calm the inflammation in her body—only her white blood cell count dropped, her liver enzymes became abnormally high, and we had to go for weekly blood draws to monitor her condition. We changed medicines again that July to Humira—a biologic—which works by targeting particular cells in the body's immune system. Accompanied by the current steroid drops, by August she was free from signs of inflammation. It's been nearly a year since then, only this time they have termed her uveitis chronic and serious.

* * *

My friendship with Stacy, Mara, and Liz solidified during our sophomore year at the University of Iowa. Stacy was our resident assistant in Daum Hall, only she seemed more like a peer than our RA. Together, we drank and smoked pot for the first time, and after a football game, when Mara passed out in her bed, we penned "virgin" on her face with a marker. We submitted a personal ad to the newspaper, seeking four men who liked Jane's Addiction and reading, and crank-called Billy Corgan of the Smashing Pumpkins when we somehow found the phone number to his Chicago home. Each of us visited Stacy's parents' farm in their small Kansas town and later, when Stacy came out, we embraced her partner as if she'd attended undergrad right alongside us.

The four of us have weathered our share of agonies from still-births to miscarriages, premature birth, infertility, and a spouse's leukemia—but there is no doubt that Stacy has had more than her share of heartache. She grew up in a conservative Christian home and her parents have not always accepted her marriage or the children who are the result of that union. Yet outwardly, Stacy remained quick with a winking quip, a hearty laugh. In my experience, such a fearless outlook was far from innate, and when hardships visited me, I gathered them up like stones and began to wall myself inside them, sinking deeper into despair. Only now, as a mom, as much as I wanted to block myself off, I discovered that the wall needed a door so that others could come and go.

\* \* \*

I pry Jolie's eyelids open with my thumb and forefinger and squeeze a drop of prednisolone into her eye. The medicine is white and as she blinks, she opens and closes her mouth, grimaces.

"That's right, you've got it," I say, encouraging her to keep blinking, to let the medicine settle deep in her eye's cavity. "You ready?" I ask, hovering over the second eye.

"Not yet," she says, dabbing her face with tissue. Sometimes she sits up and I'll rub her back before we move onto the subsequent drop. "I'm ready," she finally says and opens her unmedicated eye wide.

This brave girl. It's hard to think she's mine. Tending to her pulls me outside of my own concerns. Stacy in a hospital, Jolie on the couch, my college roommate incredulous that a good friend of ours could have a suicide plan. Liz's reaction had shocked me. At some point didn't everyone want to give up, to go away?

I recall my own such days distinctly. I wanted to write, knew it with a certainty unlike anything I had ever known. I wanted to earn my MFA, and yet despite my longings, I didn't know how to make it happen. A dutiful daughter, I'd tried nursing school like my parents wanted, and hated it. When I told my dad I wanted to write, he'd said, "That's fine, but you better get a teaching degree." I complied.

However, working in the classroom felt vastly different from story writing.

It was my third year out of college and I was living in Chicago but driving sixty miles each way to a suburban middle school where I taught seventh-grade English. This suburb was flattened by a tornado in the early '90s and developers came in and built miles of reasonably priced two-story homes overnight, complete with toothpick trees and gleaming schools. The schools of this suburb, with its shellacked veneer, could not keep up with demand, and more students were enrolled than ideal. This led to teachers like me who were without classrooms and between classes pushed carts laden with textbooks and supplies through cramped hallways.

I hated my job and I didn't know if things would ever improve. While I had been eager to share my love of literature with students, within the three years between graduating from college and working full-time, the profession lost its allure. I spent my first year teaching at a high school in central Illinois, where on my second day of class, a student told me to fuck off. During a midyear review the principal at that school noted that I would be very attractive if I lost five pounds.

During my second teaching job in the suburbs, I left my Chicago apartment at 5:30 a.m., morning dark as night, and once on I-55, I selected the left-hand lane, butted inches from the concrete meridian. Every day I thought about driving into that embankment. I was barely making rent and the other English teacher in whose room I parked my cart during third period made a point of correcting my grammar in front of my students, his eyes beady behind thick glasses, his face oily and slick. Our mutual disdain only intensified when he began leaving me notes in my mailbox that warned me not to use any of his classroom materials.

Foolishly, I approached him, asked him not to correct me in class. After that conversation he began to lock the dictionaries in a cabinet along with other supplies so my students could not use them. As things began to escalate, I asked the principal to intercede. "That's his classroom," the principal said. "I can't keep him from it. You've got to learn to work together," he said.

As I began my morning drive to the suburbs, accelerating from 50 to 65 to 70 mph, I gravitated to the left lane. By this time in my commute the car would be warm, dashboard glowing, the sound of traffic and the wind smeared windows, and I wanted to jerk the wheel to the left as hard and as fast as I could. The only thing I could hear was the voice inside my head that said: *You aren't good enough. You will never be enough. You can't you won't you shouldn't even try.*

I was certain the impact would be sufficient.

"She had a plan, Melissa. A f'ing plan."

"Oh my gosh," I said. "Poor Stacy."

Poor indeed. I think of Stacy, how she remains ready with a joke, and I wonder how long she has been fighting these thoughts. Unlike Stacy, I kept my misery to myself. It seemed easier to contain it, to replay the pointed frown of the English teacher and on the weekends, to watch friends parade in new outfits while I shopped at TJ Maxx and Goodwill. When we went out to bars, I sipped draft beer while they ordered fishbowl-sized cosmopolitans. I wanted to write, only on some level I already believed I would fail, and thinking about ending it all was the closest I could get to a reprieve. No one knew about these thoughts, but the notion sparkled in the distance, visible only to me.

* * *

My daughter looks like any other nine-year-old. She dances and swims and likes to make nests for the rabbits that dart across our backyard.

Yet every four weeks, tests that are usually administered to individuals in their seventies are administered to my fourth grader. A uveitis specialist uses a slit lamp, which emits a thin stream of light into the interior of her eye as he examines the cornea for abrasions and foreign bodies. He also looks for signs of cataracts, detached retina, and glaucoma. The tech raises the chin rest to accommodate Jolie's smaller stature.

My daughter's eyes are large and brown and almond shaped; and at this point her vision remains excellent. Yet the uveitis has no symptoms, meaning without the frequent checkups and the slit lamp there would be no way of knowing if the middle section of her eye is swollen. Ten years ago, before the introduction of biologics, the uveitis destroyed the tissue deep inside the eye, and children and adults lost their vision. The topical corticosteroids like the prednisolone are not strong enough to combat the swelling and come with their own side effects. I know we are fortunate to have health insurance, to have these drugs, to have the slit lamp and Drs. Trunger and Moorly. Not everyone has access or the means to this knowledge.

Still, we were shocked by the initial diagnosis of uveitis. Jolie doesn't wear glasses and has 20–20 vision. She's never complained of so much as a headache. Yet I'm beginning to realize it will always be like this—outwardly Jolie seems healthy. Our family is boring and mediocre. We try to eat two vegetables with our dinner. Jolie has a bedspread with butterflies and flowers; kitties in varying shades of purple pattern her lunchbox. She loves to curl up on the couch and read or cut out paper dolls of her own design, outfit them in an entire wardrobe made from scrapbook paper. But like my own knotty thoughts, there is always more going on than meets the eye.

* * *

*Sending you the biggest hug. I believe in you. I love you.* I text Stacy before the hospital staff confiscates her electronics. I watch the screen momentarily to see if she responds, then put down the phone.

I imagine they've pumped her full of drugs in an attempt to balance her moods. I last saw Stacy just a few weeks ago when the four of us convened in a hotel room in Chicago. We met in the hotel bar and ate overpriced grilled cheese sandwiches and drank wine for five hours before moving to another restaurant for more food and drinks. During that day, Stacy detailed the impending breakup with her partner of fourteen years and how days before Christmas, her partner demanded a divorce. For the majority of their marriage, Stacy had stayed home with their three children while her partner worked toward her PhD. Stacy had little money of her own and a dead résumé. Still, they had begun therapy and Stacy seemed determined to make it work. She taught adjunct and Mara had agreed to watch Stacy's kids after school.

I didn't know what had changed since our meetup in Chicago. Had her partner refused to attend therapy? Had the adjunct classes failed to fill? Or had all the variables simply become too overwhelming? What prompted her to take an idea and put it into action and conversely, what had kept me from doing the same?

Why did I keep my hands at the wheel despite their unsteadiness? How did I pull into the parking lot of Hoover Middle School and lead my students through a discussion of the novel *Children of the River*, lecturing about the Khmer Rouge, which forced thousands to flee Cambodia in the 1970s?

I woke at 4:30 a.m. to study for the GRE before driving to the suburbs. On weekends I'd sit in coffee shops around the city with a yellow legal pad and a pencil, letting a story idea unfurl and following it—the act of writing very much a pursuit of courage. And maybe that was it: the process of regularly writing and contemplating generated pure and unbridled happiness. In spite of the uncertainty of what might evolve on the page, there was also possibility. Never knowing what would appear evolved into a practice of delight.

I spent the last two periods of the day in the same classroom, where I had an actual desk alongside my cart and a small group of students lingered after the bell rang and the school day had ended.

They'd draw on the board and goof around. I was flattered by the fact that they acted as if I wasn't even there. Some were gangly and wore too-short pants. They liked Trent Reznor of Nine Inch Nails or had no idea who he was. Others dressed in all black and Doc Martens. I loved their awkwardness—loved that they chose to hang out in my classroom, their conversations lively and spiraling.

When I finally learned that I'd gotten into graduate school for writing and told these students I wouldn't be returning in the fall, I remember one of them—Erin—telling me that all year the third-period English teacher had been telling his students I was a bad teacher and they should steer clear of me.

I shrugged it off. I had gotten into graduate school and now I would have the chance to study writing. It was what I'd been working toward for months, studying for the GRE, taking a fiction-writing workshop at Columbia College Chicago, stuffing a McDonald's hamburger into my mouth on Wednesday nights minutes before class began. Maybe everyone has a plan. I had mine. I just chose not to follow it.

I'd like to put my arms around Stacy and pull her to me. I would let her know that I understand. It's hard. Today is very hard. But what tethers us to the earth today is constantly evolving and tomorrow—tomorrow may be altogether different.

How do we ever know what is to come?

Even now, life is cloaked by uncertainty. I watch Jolie blink and dab her face with a tissue. She then looks at me—her eyes like a pair of headlights leading the way through darkness.

# BARBIE STYLE HEAD

Barbie Style Head was a life-sized Barbie head with a thick coif of blonde hair that ended at her naked shoulders. My cousin Allison had a Barbie Style Head, and so did my friend Julie, but neither Allison nor Julie had the original makeup that came with the doll head. Both their moms wore the real thing—eye shadow, mascara, blush—even the tan stuff that poured from a bottle. Just seeing their moms' cosmetics lining their bathroom countertops thrilled me. Makeup made my aunt's blue eyes pop, her lips as bright and slick as licorice. And with the bodiless Barbie, I too could remake a face.

My methods for making up Barbie Style Head were always the same. I started with blush and tilted the doll head so I could better access her cheeks. I'd learned how to apply makeup by watching the women in the bathroom at the Michigan campground where we set up our pop-up camper. Some women used a darker color over their eyelids and then a lighter color beneath the brow. This was difficult to approximate on Barbie, but I made an arc of blue closest to her eye, and then rimmed a champagne color above this. I leaned back and inspected my work. No matter how hard I tried, Barbie never looked like the models on magazine covers. I spit on a tissue and wiped her face clean. It was easy enough to begin again.

I am what you would call plain. My name is Melissa but upon meeting me people usually forget and call me Michelle. I'm five feet eight with brown hair and brown eyes. There isn't anything memorable about my looks. I have the long Roman nose from the Sicilian side of my family that concludes with a generous pad of skin, like putty jammed over the end of a pipe. I would never call myself beautiful, but with makeup I've always felt that a certain potential exists. The tricky thing is I am also the mother to two daughters, so everything I do and say carries extra weight. If I wear makeup, what am I potentially telling my daughters about the importance of their looks? If I forbid cosmetics, will my daughters be any more empowered?

My mother penciled in her eyebrows and on Sunday dashed a lipstick across her mouth before church, but that was the extent of her makeup wearing. She was too busy being a den mother and scout leader, working 3:00 p.m. to 11:00 p.m. shifts as a nurse at St. Margaret's. I once found a gold-etched compact in her medicine cabinet and when I asked her about it she said she used it during formal dances Dad took her to when she was in nursing school.

The compressed powder was a pale pink, like the inside of an ear, and smelled faintly of cornflakes. But there were places where the bottom of the compact shone through. I imagined Mom gliding across a dance floor, Dad's arm around her back.

Makeup was part of this allure. A woman had the face she was born with, but the creams and powders, wands and tubes could make that same face into something new—a critical opportunity.

Sometimes Dad commented that a woman on TV or in a movie looked attractive, and one time my grandma, his mom, said that if a man stopped looking at women, he was dead. I didn't question a man's right to evaluate a woman for her appearance, and in doing so I gathered the importance of looks.

If I could make Barbie pretty, surely I could do the same with myself.

Growing up in a working-class suburb of Chicago, anything I did inside or outside of school could be described as mediocre at best.

But when I walked the makeup aisle at Hotz Drugs, an undeniable whip of excitement tore through me. The packages of shiny plastic tubes dangled from shelves like little soldiers. As I dug through a rack, I thought of my junior high crush liking me back; I imagined a report card with all As and the most popular girls inviting me to sleepovers. With makeup, I could not just fit in but excel.

Makeup encourages homogeny. It wasn't until the 1970s that cosmetic companies began to offer makeup for darker skin tones. Barbie Style Head with her bouncy blonde hair and blue eyes embraced just one version of beauty that as a child I failed to question. Toys like the Barbie Style Head are built on hope—the plastic carefully molded into a shaky sense of self, one for whom improvement is always possible and perfection an application away.

I never disputed Barbie's popularity or my fascination with her. She's been around since 1959. Ninety-nine percent of three-to-ten-year-old girls own a Barbie doll. I owned several. But when I later learn her shape was actually based on a German doll called Lili, a prostitute gag gift distributed at bachelor parties, I wondered who decided to mass-produce these dolls and market them to little girls. When my daughters came of age, I refused to purchase the dolls for them. I hoped that they might tap into their minds and hearts rather than develop an objectified view of their bodies. Maybe the toys they played with would make a difference.

I've heard it before: if the traditional Barbie doll were a real woman, she would be five feet nine and weight a hundred twenty pounds. Her body fat would be so low she would be unable to menstruate. Yet Mattel, the toy company that makes Barbie, claims that Barbie's proportions were created for ease of dressing, not to replicate the female figure.

I don't know if such studies are what prompts a change, but in 2016 Mattel introduced Fashionistas, a line of dolls with an array of body types—tall, petite, and curvy. During the release a company spokesperson explained that the new dolls would provide "a better reflection of what girls see in the world around them."

I wonder: *What about the sixty-one years before now?*

The truth is that I feel most beautiful when my face is not part of the equation. I'm prettiest when I'm paddling in Minnesota's Boundary Waters, running trails near our house, or driving close to the end of an essay. So maybe it isn't that makeup exists, but that I feel a need to wear it.

I'm not ready unless I've dabbed on concealer or etched a few lines where my eyebrows have thinned. I never feel secure in my own skin. I can't walk by a mirror without looking at it, curious about what everyone else sees. It is as if I am waiting for a glitzy, glamorous fairy godmother, someone to gently take my face in her hands and complete me.

My own daughters sailed through elementary school without much of a glance at Barbie or my beloved Barbie Style Head. When they had their first dance recital and we were instructed to put makeup on them, Eva squirmed in her seat as I smoothed gobs of foundation on her cheeks.

"It itches," she complained, and after returning home, the first thing she did was march to the bathroom and scrub her face. It made me hopeful that some of my complicated issues of self-image may not be passed down. My other daughter, Jolie, has a chronic eye condition, and every few weeks we drive an hour from our home to see a specialist in Indianapolis. In the darkened exam room, before peering into her eyes, the first thing the doctor says to her is, "Why, it's the prettiest patient I've seen all day!"

The first few times I countered that she was also the smartest. The ophthalmologist didn't respond and still repeats the same comment, like he has some recording inside himself and each time he sees us he hits the "play" button.

Maybe he feels the need to say something complimentary and a comment about her looks is the easiest offer.

Still, I've begun to pretend I don't hear this greeting.

The girls are ten years old now. This fall I've been reading Lucy Grealy's *Autobiography of a Face* to them at bedtime. The book recounts how the author, who had part of her face removed due to an Ewing's sarcoma, endures countless surgeries in an attempt to reconstruct her face. The book has riveted my daughters because Grealy was first diagnosed with cancer in the fourth grade, their current class.

"Wait!" Jolie said, tipping the book from my hands to peer at Grealy's picture on the back jacket. "I think she's beautiful," she said. "But it's so sad."

"What's so sad?" I asked.

"How much she hates herself."

I could only nod.

The fact is I'd like to be makeup-free like my own mother. I'd like to show my daughters that who I am is enough—only wanting this does not make it reality. I don't imagine that reading Grealy's book will infuse my daughters with a stronger sense of self, but perhaps learning about her struggle can provide perspective about their own developing perceptions.

I can still remember the cabinet in the basement corner where my cousin kept her Barbie Style Head. I'd sit on the carpet, situate the Barbie between my legs, and assess her features. I turned her face from one side to the other, and then sorted through the Ziploc that held my aunt's old makeup. There were pots of blush and squares of eyeshadow in a range of blues and greens and less-desirable browns. One visit, my sister and cousin joined me on the floor and we took turns making up the Barbie.

My sister did the eyes while my cousin worked on the hair; I added blush and tried to moisten her plastic lips with the gummed end of a lip gloss wand. When we finished, Barbie looked like she was ready to take the center stage of a carnival. Multiple ponytails and barrettes batted down her hair. The space above her plastic eyes sparkled blue, an arch of color that continued into her hairline. Goo smeared her lips outside their natural lines like a bouquet of flowers had bloomed on her face all at once. We giggled, delighted by our combined work, oblivious to the fact that the rest of Barbie was absent.

# MY BODY, MY SHAME

My husband tells my daughters about my adolescent eating disorder on a random Wednesday as I'm scooping stir-fry over rice. This halts my spoon mid-air. Eva has said she's not hungry, though she just finished two hours of ballet on pointe and after school only ate a small bowl of milk-soggy cereal.

"Your mother dieted so hard when she was your age that she stopped having periods for two years," Pete says.

The early autumn breeze kicks open the curtains, then they collapse into limpness.

I glance at my husband, hoping to catch his eye. *I never said you could tell them*, I want to say. *That was never yours to tell*, I imagine saying later, when it's just the two of us—but already it feels too late.

"You've got to eat," I say. "If you think you need to stay thin to dance, the dancing will go away. That's a promise."

Eva's mouth opens in silent protest, but her brows furrow. I feel righteous, despite all that has changed in the past three months: the new junior high with its electives, Eva's backpack a granite of books, the cafeteria lunch—mozzarella sticks! Pasta bar! And she's only a few inches shy of me. I vibrate under the bright kitchen lights, electrified by the words I've spoken. The truth is I'm fed up with the weekend dance rehearsals and nightly practices. This is our first dinner together in days. I keep my face firm, place a generous bowl in front of her.

I feel sticky, as if his words had coated me in syrup. I've never told them how in junior high, the same age Eva and her twin sister are now, I restricted my calories to the very minimum, eating a slice of dry toast for breakfast, a salad blanketed with cold cuts at lunch, a few bites from a mealy apple that I thunked in the classroom trash-can. I feel exposed, as if they've all just been transported to my child-hood bedroom with its reversible striped comforter from Venture and glossy homage to Rob Lowe and Rick Schroder. They are there to witness what I do each day after school, sometimes twice a day.

Pete has put them there.

There's the white roll-top desk where I do my homework, a can-ister of pencils with a tiny blue square of paper with equations I'm trying to memorize. On the other side of the room is a vanity with a mirror and stool where I keep my hairbrush and the few cosmetics I own.

I never asked for the vanity, but received it for my thirteenth birthday. Anytime I sat at the vanity I didn't know what to do except look at myself, which reminded me of *Girl at Mirror*, the Norman Rockwell painting of a girl with fisted hands on either side of her chin, a folded-over magazine with a close-up of a movie star in her lap. The girl was not much older than me and sat in her slip, wearing the same expression I felt sitting before the vanity: one of scorn and frustration—unsure who or what I saw, or worse, worried that who others saw was vastly different from how I might be perceived.

I felt wholly inadequate at thirteen and dieting became an easy way for me to execute some control.

Only it didn't end with food. Each day after school I'd lock the door to my room, line up my ankles, and examine the tops of my thighs to make sure they did not touch. Then I'd sprawl on the floor and do leg lifts and tummy crunches.

I see the adolescent me stretched out on the rug and my face warms. Now, at age forty-eight, as I sit at the dinner table, stomach puffing over the waistband of my old jeans, I'm certain that's who my family sees.

"It's true," I say. "I dieted so much that my periods stopped, and my hair thinned. Now I keep getting stress fractures. Do you want to ask me about it?"

But what is *it*? Exactly what did Pete just share? Anorexia? I was never hospitalized. My parents never threatened me at mealtimes. I ate a normal dinner, just less, and once I realized I'd never have breasts until I gained weight, I reversed course, packing on pounds. I made brownies from a box, Rice Krispies treats, peach cobbler with canned fruit from the pantry.

When they don't say anything, I ask my daughters again. "Do you have any questions?"

"No?" says Eva, hesitation in her voice as she tilts her face to the side.

My husband inquires about today's math test. Our chopsticks twitch as we pick up tofu I've chopped and baked, only it tastes empty, like we're all eating seasoned air.

I've used my body to carry my daughters and feed them—must I also disclose all of my adolescent shame?

Will I someday have to recount how my first date ended with a boy parking five houses down from my own and then proceeding to paw me like a puppy? Or the time my summer swim coach pulled me into the water after our last meet of the summer and pressed himself against me? I wanted to impress others, men in particular, and had placed their needs and wants before my own. Dieting had been a way for me to try to meet their unspoken expectations.

I look at Eva again. She is a rule follower, leans on the anxious side, and is quick to cry. At the height of the pandemic, I'd find her holed up in her room with the blinds drawn, crying. The tears would last for hours. I'd touch her back. "Can you tell me what's wrong? I can't help you unless I know."

After what seemed like days, she spoke. "I just don't like myself."

How to let her know I had sometimes felt this way at twelve and twenty-two and now, in my late forties?

"Just because you think something, doesn't mean it's true." Eva blinked and something rippled through me. It was what I wish I had been told. Eva hugged me hard and fast. It felt powerful all the same.

Maybe in order for her to understand her own feelings, she needs to see me grappling with things that even now confuse and embarrass me.

Later, when Pete and I are cleaning the kitchen and the girls are showering, I speak up. "I never told that to the girls. About my eating." The words sound tiny and compact, and I like how contained they feel in my mouth.

"You can't assume that your issues are going to become theirs," he says. "Did you see Eva's face? She really loves dance. Maybe she just wasn't hungry."

*Did* I see her face, really? I had been focused on my adolescent self. But it was true: when I threatened to put an end to ballet, her bright face turned shadowy.

That night Eva and her sister pile ice cream into bowls and add a deluge of chocolate syrup, laughing as they drizzle squiggles on their fingers and lick it away. Pete and I stand together and watch. Their appetites feed me, dare me to continue telling my truths.

# TO MY TEEN DAUGHTERS: YOU DON'T OWE THE "CREEPY GUY" ANYTHING

I do not act alarmed when I overhear my daughters talking about the creepy guy. It's a Friday night and I am picking up them and their two friends from the outdoor ice rink. A Christmas song tinkles in the background.

"There he is," says one of my daughters' friends.

"Ugh," says the other.

I slow the car and look off in the direction they point. A man in a puffy beige coat with hands in his pockets and baggy corduroys slinks off with another guy, stepping over the curb onto the sidewalk, moving past the CD store in the direction of the movie theater with its garish marquee.

From our car, he looks unassuming and unthreatening and even so, my anxiety escalates.

"I don't know," says Eva. "Maybe he just wanted to talk."

"No," says Jolie, my other daughter. "He was following us."

And the pit in my stomach, maybe the one that's been there since the doctor announced thirteen years ago that I had just given birth to twin girls, triples.

"Well, you stayed together," I say, laying down each word like a life raft. "That's the best thing you can do. Normally if someone like that gives you a hard time, as long as you stay together, you should be okay." At the corner, I make my turn and we sail past the creepy guy.

My daughters are at an age where they don't tell me much and even what they do share is vague or delivered begrudgingly, so I learn by chauffeuring them and their friends. In the car, the girls open up.

As I listen, I discover a wave of nostalgia for my own seventh-grade experiences with my best friend, how we'd shop weekly in downtown Lansing, spend our babysitting money on used paperback books and lip gloss from Ben Franklin, then lunch on pizza and slices of pie from Baker's Square.

At the end of the day, if the weather were nice, we'd walk the two miles to my friend's house. We'd be talking about school, movies we wanted to see, maybe trying out a few lyrics to the latest song by A-ha, when a sudden blare of a car horn would stop us. The first few times it happened, it set my heart racing, and I'd look to my friend.

*What were you saying?* I might ask, and we'd slip back into conversation. Somehow we came to assume that if we were out and about in public, there would be interruptions like this. Catcalls, I later learned they were called.

*Boys will be boys*, the teachers said when someone complained about them snapping the backs of our bras during recess, or Anna, the most developed of anyone in our class, tired of the song a group of boys sang to her: "Put your head on my boulder . . . ," sung to the tune of the Head and Shoulders jingle.

After a day trapped in the musty yellow walls of our school, there was nothing I enjoyed more than having a snack and then hopping on my bike and riding it through the forest preserve. During much of the ride, the path snaked behind trees, but when I came to Glenwood Dyer Road, I needed to bike along the street, a two-lane stretch with only a narrow spit of gravel; my heartbeat ramped up before I even began.

Then I sped as fast as I could, stomach clenching at the sound of each approaching car, waiting for the shriek of a horn, whistles and jeers, *Hey baby!* from passing pickups. Sometimes hands and arms would fly out open windows as if I were a bird for catching, and I'd will my bicycle—and me—to stay upright.

I bent further, pedaled harder, aware of myself in a way I hadn't been in the preceding moments. The older I got, the more I came to expect that if I ventured outside, some guy would whistle, reminding me that I was a girl, and being a girl meant sex, something of which I had only a vague understanding.

Afterward, at home in my room with the pile of stuffed animals nested against the wall of my bed, I felt a heightened awareness of myself, my body secured, safely out of sight.

As the girls move on from their spills on the ice to their blisters, the vent a hot nozzle blazing my shins, I'm thinking about the creepy guy and my response. Did I just insinuate that he would be just the first of many creepy guys? Did I tell the girls to expect creepy guys, and then accept them?

A few years ago, two teens in a nearby town were abducted and murdered while out walking trails near their homes. And before them, there were other girls and young women in towns large and small—girls with legs that pushed bicycle pedals and balanced on ice skates—or dashed frantically through the woods, knees lifted, breath torn and raging out of their chests.

My daughters and their friends with their gleaming hair and porcelain skin, laugh freely, as girls do when they are together. It is just the four of them and I am a mother.

I was once a girl just like them and maybe they sense it; still, I want to pull the car over and turn on the overhead lights, my forty-eight-year-old face lit up before them.

"I was wrong," I'll say. "You don't owe him anything—not a smile, not a nice word, or even a 'no thank you.'" I want to break this cycle of accepting that as girls they are objects of desirability.

I'd like to think there is still a role for me as my daughters become women and I urge them to raise their voices, hold a gaze, and take up space. Later, at the kitchen table over hot tea for one, hot chocolate for the other, I ask my daughters, "That creepy guy. What did he say? Did he try to get you to go somewhere with him?"

"He just kept talking to us," says Jolie.

"Well, what he did wasn't right," I say. "You don't have to put up with any of that."

"We know," they say, and look to the clock on the wall.

The moment, it seems, has passed. Meanwhile, the creepy guy walks freely.

I look down at my hands, remember how they steadied myself during afternoon bike rides, delighted to be outside with the wind on my face after a long day of classes, sun a warm hand on my back. Feeling free and alive in the deep woods, breath strumming in and out and, for a moment, more than a girl.

# UNDER-PRESCRIBED

That Easter would be the last egg hunt. Dad stood silent on the patio, white hair dithering, watching my daughters and their cousin jet from one side of the yard to the other: "Found one!" they shouted, the braces on their teeth glinting, scooping up plastic eggs the same color as the foil-wrapped pots of lilies that decorated the altar of St. Ann's, where as a child I fixated on the white linen painting of the just-resurrected Jesus resplendent in white robes, a golden globe framing his head, arms extended, the holes in his palms simple brown circles. *Shouldn't they be red?* I thought. I was certain that the real Jesus—the son of God—lived behind the fabric of the painting, which somehow led to our basement beside the hot water tank and gurgling sump pump, Dad's rifles in their padded cases—a sort of tunnel that connected Jesus from the painting to the innards of our house, keeping us safe.

Only I knew he was there.

The girls spent the day in the basement sewing clothes for a green and white calico rabbit they called Ratty, the three of them stitching by hand under bars of blazing light as muffled sounds from upstairs filtered down: the barking dogs, clattering baking dishes, my mother's shuffled steps. Behind them shelves heaved with oversized items from Costco: oatmeal, pretzels, paper towels, things my parents use, only who knew what this year would hold; no one talked about it, the sky flushed and rosy. We had yet to eat the kapusta, creamy cabbage hunked with Polish sausage, but we were all waiting to hear the results of Dad's biopsy and he was quiet. He didn't talk until later, after dinner, when someone spied a wet spot on the living room rug from one of the dogs. I started cleaning dishes from the table; the food all had the same lukewarm flavor and as I held the stacked plates in my arms, I passed Dad bent over, dabbing the wetness with a folded-over paper towel, a dark splotch blooming on his jeans, at the back of his thigh, an odd place. Did he sit in the dog's urine? A thwap of panic hit me and once I saw it I couldn't unsee it; he had surgery some years ago for prostate cancer and it changed some things unknown to me until now, and later, on the long drive back on US-41, newly painted signs for Trump 2024, sun drooping in cursory orange shadows, my daughters' devices brightening the backseat, the signs for the speed limit appeared smudged. I squinted and the telephone poles lengthened, the billboards crisp. It was an old trick I used to see the chalkboard until sixth grade when it was my turn to read the sentence on the film strip and the whole thing remained fuzzy and indistinct, and Mrs. Pamlis announced I needed glasses, so I breathed through my mouth to keep from crying. I already saw things that others did not, like how Jesus had shown himself to me and for a while I had believed, and now at the optometrist for the third time in two months, I confess everything is blurry. He clicks a few slides on the phoropter and shows me my vision with a stronger prescription.

*I actually like to be under-prescribed*, he says, and I think of the hazy street signs, the invisible stitches my daughters made with their cousin, Dad bent over, cleaning up the dog's mess, the phone call that hadn't yet arrived, its cold ring coming after all of us had left and it's just the two of them again, my parents, and Dad picks up, says hello.

# DIABETIC VERNACULAR

Emily and I once sang as loud as we could to songs by The Cure and U2 and REM, hands elbows shoulders jimmying to the music as I drove us to swim practice and to the mall and parties in the soft maroon seats of my Chevy. I delighted in Emily's falling-down world. That she could not find her sunglasses, excavated scrunched up bills from her pockets, wasn't sure where she'd put her driver's license. Sometimes Emily picked me up in her car, although I lived farther from the rest of our friends, like driving to Lansing was some concession that she alone had been willing to undertake, and I was grateful for her generosity, the stick shift she drove a magical practiced dance.

Now we are both adults and moms. Emily and I are only able to see each other a few times a year. We meet halfway between our homes at the Panera on US-30, then jump into her Prius and drive to a trail beside a winding road dotted with condos. I don't even know the name of the street and I love this about our gatherings: that the streets here have no names.

Inside her car there's a blanket over the backseat to protect it from her dog; her son's basketball rolls on the floor, an empty bottle of a sports drink with a few blue dregs. As she drives, I tell her which way to turn, because she's never been good with directions. Near her, everything loosens and I feel sixteen again, the two of us road-tripping to Illinois State to spend the night with Emily's college-aged friend. During the trip we snacked from a bag of M&Ms although diabetics aren't supposed to have candy. But sometimes her blood sugar would dip, so she'd eat half a cookie or granola bar or M&Ms. Plain. With Emily, simply eating became outrageous and daring.

\* \* \*

The summer before senior year, we both lifeguarded at Crestview Pool, where at night we broke all the rules.

Jason or Katy would lock the pool gate, turn up the music on the speakers as a strip of orange blurred the horizon and bugs plinked the illuminated boxes overhead. There was no way to increase flow on the waterslide, but after sunset, the white gush at the end of the slide seemed to triple, and we shouted over the roar as we flung ourselves down the slide right after each other, dove headfirst from the shallow end. One time in the pool's diving well we greased a watermelon so it would be difficult to grasp, divided into teams, and worked to push the watermelon to the opponent's side, like water polo, only with fruit.

Curlicues of light skittered across the waves, water rolling up to our chins as we bobbed and stretched and kicked in the viscous warmth. The chlorine burned off by then, so it was easy to think I was somewhere else. The hulk of melon sailing by my thighs could be a fish, some scaled, nameless beast. When I felt its bulk haze past me, I let myself imagine for a moment that some watery terror had arrived. What would I do as it pulled me down? There was a sort of delight in imagining danger in the slick chemical water because I knew I was safe. We were the only living things that could survive in the pool, our young legs motoring us upright.

We could go on like this for hours.

That summer Emily called to tell me two other lifeguards had done it in the pump room. "Fly with me," is what Jason said to Anita. I sat on my bed, the vinyl blinds flicking back and forth inside the bedroom window. I pushed my face closer until my lips nearly touched the screen. I didn't want anyone to hear. Coolness rose from the shaded grass while a quick gust of wind flicked a tongue of sun-warmed air, harbinger of the day's sticky pulse. I'd slept in. Mid-morning already clammy and hot. Our shifts at the pool didn't begin until after lunch. I let the gravity of what she said wash over me. *It*. We were obsessed with *it*. Losing it. Doing it.

"Oh my gosh," I said. "I can't believe it." I still couldn't quite grasp what went where or how. Where had they placed their towels? Or had they remained standing? These were the stories we liked best. We were both virgins, and neither one of us had any prospects otherwise, but we were intrigued by the choices others made. By the summer's end Heather had also done it in the pump room with Jason, and anytime I went in there for the kit to test the pool's chemicals, I moved quietly, reverently, as if desecrating a holy place.

The chlorine pump droned on, the industry of water churning beneath the concrete floor, its vibration a somnolent hum. How could Jason even hear her response?

\* \* \*

Emily lives north of Chicago, about two and a half hours from me, ideal for a weekend visit, only this seldom happens. There is ballet rehearsal, or lately, visits to help my parents during my dad's illness.

It's been years since the Halloween when Emily and her son, Sam, slept over. The girls were in kindergarten, and Sam chased them and the other kids with a wooden gun (I think he was a pirate?) and when our entourage made its way up and down the sidewalk, Sam kept pushing over Halloween decorations, running circles on the lawn. We hooted. Who wasn't amped up on sugar that night? Then when I went to draw the girls a bath, Emily wanted to put Sam in there with them. I thought she was joking. I shook my head, no, said that there wouldn't be enough room. I tried to laugh, waited for her to join me. *He's a boy*, I thought. *It's not the same.* The fact that we believed differently surprised me.

* * *

At the pool, Jon served up Polish dogs and nachos in little plastic boats, bags of popcorn and Styrofoam cups of soda pop. He asked me out on a napkin, tucked it beneath my car's wipers.

Later that summer at a party, after we'd been dating for several weeks, Jon kissed me. It wasn't the first time we kissed but we were new enough that I was still getting to know him, the two of us stretched out on the kitchen linoleum, everyone from the pool lurking and twisted up in different rooms. The lights were off. I pressed against him and felt a thundering between my legs. Kissing him, my breath flushed stumpy, inefficient. At one point he pulled back and whispered that he was falling in love with me. I would understand if he said it quickly, tossing the words out there in hopes of gaining access to the rest of my body, but he said it with meaning, his voice deep and serious. I thought he was crazy. "Don't," I said. By then I had stopped believing good things were meant for me. "I'll only hurt you." And it felt like a generous thing to do: to warn him about me.

* * *

One October day, Emily and I have only just begun our walk on the trail, have barely finished telling each other about our mornings and the traffic we'd encountered, when I notice Emily is walking crooked. Then she bops into me without apologizing. "Is your sugar low?"

"No," Emily says. "It's fine."

"Do you have a granola bar?" I ask.

Emily says she does and we continue walking. But I feel the familiar edge, my own alertness, duty bound, even though she never asked this of me. In high school she sometimes let me pick out a freckle on her left bicep and then she'd hand me the insulin-filled syringe. Afterward I'd ask, *Did it hurt?*

Emily had more friends clamoring around her locker at school. She was in the harder math class and when she swam, she seemed to always improve her time. I could not compete with her and had no desire to do so. But I could ask her about her blood sugar and, by virtue of my questions and preening, I created a role for myself. Reminding Emily about her diabetes became one of my jobs, like keeping a secret or offering advice about a boy.

The wind flips the collar of my jacket. I straighten it and look at Emily. Her eyes are steady, hands even. I am relieved. There's so much to catch up on.

"How's your dad?" she asks.

I tell her how he's finished with chemotherapy and radiation to his head and neck, but that he's lost so much weight that he looks like a war survivor. Emily's a physician, so I can't help but hope she has some suggestions for his weakness, the weight loss, his inability to take in much more than Ensure. Only there isn't anything she or anyone can offer. It's just going to take time. "Are your folks okay?" I ask.

"My dad can't hear," she says. "And he refuses to wear his hearing aid. I go over there and have to yell to talk with him." We both laugh a bit even though it isn't funny. It's nice to talk about our parents, just like we did when they annoyed us in high school.

We move onto our kids. Sam is in eighth grade. My twin daughters are in seventh. "I never see them anymore," I tell her. "They come home from school, grab a snack, then go into their rooms." I share with her how we've begun to refer to their rooms as their apartments. She says it's the same thing with Sam, and we walk in silence for a few beats.

"I mean, I remember in high school my parents asking me questions and stuff and maybe not wanting to answer them, but I did," she says. Suddenly rap music erupts out of Emily's rear. She stops and pats her pockets, then finds her phone and shuts it off. "Butt dial," she says. Emily pushes the phone in her back pocket. But doesn't move. The paved trail extends before us, cuts through a field, then is flanked by woods on either side. "You're walking so fast," she says. "You've got those long legs." And now I see that she's breathing hard. "Can we slow down?"

I smile. Our difference in height, like so many other attributes, unchanged.

*  *  *

I first visited Emily's house sometime during our freshman year of high school. Emily's sisters watched TV from the couch as the two of us rushed into her bedroom and shut the door. Her wood-paneled room was right off the garage and across from the small bathroom where later in high school we'd smooth our lips with gloss before heading out for the night. She had a canopy bed and above the headboard had taped pictures of Janet Evans, the famed Olympic swimmer. She was only a few years older than us and we loved the idea that someone so close in age could end up in the Olympics. Beside this Emily's own swimming medals and ribbons hung from nails. Emily excelled at butterfly and freestyle, and when she raced at meets, it seemed like she was having fun.

We flipped through magazines and talked about boys. Emily had a crush on a guy from her algebra class and I was still thinking about Coach Matt, my swim coach from the previous summer. I didn't tell Emily about him, but his memory spun close as I walked the halls at school or attended Friday night football games, looking for an approximation of him. It wasn't love, I knew that, but the way he had frightened me needed to mean something.

Emily's dad worked the baggage claim at Midway Airport and tossed suitcases and duffle bags onto the conveyor belt snaking behind the check-in counter. Both of our moms were nurses. They packed us fruit when we had weekend swim invitationals. Emily's mom always said I was responsible. That might be true, but Emily was the generous one. Just last month she welcomed a high school classmate to take up residence in her sunroom after the classmate divorced her husband and had nowhere to go. Sophomore year I was in a particular funk and between classes Emily handed me a pocket-sized poem by John Greenleaf Whittier. She had slid it inside a triangle-folded note:

> When things go wrong, as they sometimes will,
> When the road you're trudging seems all uphill,
> When the funds are low and the debts are high,
> And you want to smile, but you have to sigh,
> When care is pressing you down a bit,
> Rest, if you must, but don't you quit.

The words of the poem were printed in a soft teal and the card itself a silver metallic, and if I turned it in my hand, it sparkled. I kept the poem in my wallet for years. I think I was getting by with a C in biology, or maybe that wasn't it at all. Maybe the boy I was crushing on had begun to date someone else. Or maybe it was the fact my sister, an eighth grader, was carpooling with us in the morning so she could attend an accelerated math class at my high school. It would always set me off, how she was able to hand over yet another accomplishment to my parents and they in turn wore such achievements like prized medallions. I never expressed these things about my family but on some level, Emily seemed to sense it. She was always telling me to hang in there. From anyone else, such a reminder might have annoyed me. It wasn't cool to admit any wants about one's parents beyond a desire for them to leave us alone. But deep inside, I did want better grades. I did want to feel like I belonged. Emily knew this. And her knowing gave me the closest thing I had to confidence.

\* \* \*

The building that housed the changing rooms, the concessions stand, the lifeguards' lockers—is gone. The pool and waterslide and pump room. All of it demolished. Although it's been close to thirty years since we worked there, we still talk about Crestview Pool. And how Scott would tell the kids who'd been there since opening to go home and Anita with her colored contacts (aqua! Lilac!) would buy gyros from Rosie's and smack her lips when something disgusted her; Harry worked part-time for his dad's plumbing company; Jon and Nick fielded concessions. Brandon had that concave bone that protruded from his chest. He marched around in a red ballcap, twirling his whistle. Sometimes we called him Super Guard and laughed at him behind his back. At Crestview, we tried out adulthood. We reminded the kids to walk, not run, to wait until the diver swam to the ladder before cannonballing off the springboard. We outwardly embraced the speech of safety so that they might play again the next day; beneath the scorching sun, it seemed that none of it would ever end.

\* \* \*

Emily found joy with ease and maybe I considered her luckier for it. Who didn't want to be around someone so fun? On more than one occasion I would be shopping with Mom or running an errand and a stranger—a man I did not know—might say, *Hey! It's not that bad! Smile!* And then I'd grin widely, self-consciously berating myself. Why wasn't I smiling? What *was* so bad? I needed to work harder at happiness. I wanted to be liked. I wanted to please others even if it meant being dishonest with myself. No one was talking about depression in those days, but looking back, I was depressed, returning from school and undressing, slipping beneath the covers of my bed, the smooth touch of the sheets on my bare legs, sleeping until dinner or swim practice or whatever arrived first.

Junior year, Emily dated Tim. The two of them were always cracking each other up. I loved seeing her happy, listening to her laughter, which seemed different from how other girls laughed, even me. I wasn't dating anyone, so for Turnabout dance, I asked a senior I didn't know to go with me. He was on the basketball team and stood a head taller than me. I really didn't know much more than his name and that was the fun of it: I'd asked a boy I didn't know—and he'd said yes.

I don't remember dancing with my date. I don't remember him smiling at me or even saying my name.

I don't remember Emily and Tim giving me a ride home that night. Why had I gone to a dance with a boy I didn't know? Why had I smiled when I didn't feel like it?

"Melissa, you threw yourself at him," Emily later said, unknowingly. Had I?

\* \* \*

"It's going to be a miracle if he graduates high school," Emily says about her son. "Stop that," I say. "He's going to be fine." We are both challenged by our kids. As we walk, we share our concerns. I tell Emily how I drove one of my daughters' friends home recently and learned more about seventh grade during the ten-minute drive than anything my own girls have shared. But I don't tell Emily how lonely I feel around them, like they have died and it's only their ghosts inhabiting their clothes, using the same toothbrushes, fighting over the use of a reusable straw at dinner. There are other worries. Both our dads have had prostate cancer and Emily's mom recently had surgery. As much as I want to talk about the girls, I remain quiet. Emily's words are more urgent. Just last week Sam had sat at his social studies teacher's desk when she was out of the room and typed something disrespectful on her computer.

"What happened?" I asked.

"She sent him to the office."

Our kids are different. Emily's son loves skateboarding and basketball. Expensive high-tops. My girls dance ballet on pointe. When I play pop music in the car, they turn it down.

"Don't you like this song?" I'll ask.

They shrug. "Not really."

When Pete had back surgery Emily offered to come help and take care of the girls, but I demurred. Sitting down to a meal with Pete and the girls, walking the dog together on a Sunday feels as divine as I imagine it must have been to be surrounded at your locker by high school classmates or succeed in the most challenging classes. I am a different person around Emily and Pete and the few times we've all been together have left me unsettled.

\* \* \*

*What qualities about the applicant do you believe would make them a good parent?* I read the question for the adoption paperwork on my laptop while pumping breast milk in the middle of the night. We were living in Evergreen Park then. The girls were a few months old and sleep a veiny thing I longed for. How I moved in a haze throughout the day—a cycle of diapering, nursing, changing, throwing load after load of wash. I couldn't put it off any longer. I'd agreed to be a personal reference for Emily. She planned to submit the paperwork to adopt a child from Latvia before they changed the guidelines. It was one of the few countries that permitted single-parent adoption. I was still new enough at parenthood that I didn't give this a second thought. If anyone could be a successful parent, it was Emily.

I wore a hands-free pumping bra, a vest with a zipper down the front and two holes where the suction cups fitted against my breasts and sucked my flesh into cones like Madonna during her *Like a Prayer* years.

The breast pump whirred. A soft yellow light glowed from the alley out back. Every so often a gust rose up, twirled the shadowed branches of the tree like whisks on a beater. It was one or two in the morning and later tiny spackles of milk shadowed my screen.

I talked about how I'd known her since we were fourteen and she was kind and generous with a kryptonite sense of honor. I typed as much as would fit in the box.

* * *

There was the time after college when Emily was living in Chicago and she didn't answer her phone and her mom called the police and they had to break into her apartment, wake her up, give her juice.

There was the time we were in Paris, walking along the Seine at night and footsteps clomped behind us, grew closer and closer until we took off, running as hard and fast as we could, a container of Mace in my hand.

There was the time when we were high schoolers visiting Emily's friend at Illinois State, attending a party in the basement of a fraternity house, music pounding. *What? What?* We said into each other's ears, the ceiling low and sticky, how sweat dotted the back of my neck, the skin above Emily's lip. Two guys poured us Hi-C mixed with Everclear and after a while told us to follow them upstairs. They were showing us their room with the lofted beds when Emily's friend caught up with us, grabbed our arms, and led us back to her dorm. We didn't have coats and hugged our arms as we walked across campus, our breath faceless phantoms. "You don't go into a guy's room," Emily's friend admonished, shaking her head. "Ever."

Researchers say that memory is faulty, that each time we return to an event, we bring not just recollection but our interpretation. Maybe such memories offer a chance to remind us how far we've come.

Sometimes when I start writing I have a general idea of where I'm headed, but it hasn't come to me until now that writing about Emily is a way for us to be together in the manner we once were, trying out different versions of ourselves.

* * *

I tried to talk to Emily but she wasn't following, eyes wild buzzy things. For years I had been there when her balance became shaky, her words garbled, so when it happened on the train in Naples, Italy, it shouldn't have been a big deal. We were new college graduates and the plan was to take a late afternoon boat to Capri where we'd reserved two nights in the back room of a woman's home, breakfast included. Neither one of us spoke Italian, but I understood Emily's own diabetic vernacular, her words thick as glue, how she slouched so much on the train that she was nearly sideways, spilling into the empty seat next to her. I unzipped the pouch at my waist, unwrapped the vial of glucose tabs her mom had handed me before we left the United States. I placed one in Emily's hand, told her to eat it. Didn't think she would do anything but what I asked. Instead, Emily flung the tab out of my hand, sent it sailing down the sooty aisle.

Nearly everyone had left the train at that point and the voice on the speaker overhead announced the next departure. "We need to go," I said, and grabbed Emily's arm, steered her toward the exit, dragging the straps of our bags behind me. She was surly and groaned, shaking her head back and forth. She took three steps out of the train onto the station, the black asphalt gummed my shoes in the late June heat. I kept a hand on one of Emily's shoulders, but then she twisted away from my grasp, aimed herself away from me, only she couldn't run or walk straight, her feet crisscrossed. "Emily!" I yelled and darted after her, this time grabbing her from the backside, arms circling her shoulders, chin knocking her head; I slid another pink disk into my palm. Blood ticked in my ears.

"Let me go," she said, dangling over my forearms, and then I pushed the tab into her mouth, clamped a hand over her lips.

"*Ayuda!*" I yelled, my high school Spanish the closest approximation to Italian. She kept trying to walk, feet colliding, gradually slowing, her body slanted the other direction until she tipped over my arms like a toy that had run out of batteries.

By the time the men in uniforms arrived with their medical bag, the tab dissolved along with her fight. I pointed at Emily. "*No sucre?*" I said.

They spoke Italian, which I did not understand. They looked at each other, and then one of them ran off for juice.

When it was all over, we hoisted our packs onto our backs, tightened the straps and headed toward the station's exit. My shirt starched with sweat, legs and back as achy as if I'd run a marathon. Emily handed the plastic cup to me. "Want some?"

She never acted like the close calls; the danger was anything but a hiccup. Nothing could stop her, and so we didn't talk about it and I never brought it up, but in later years I'd replay how I called out for help and they'd come. It had been my voice.

* * *

Our visit ends where it began, at the Panera where I've left my car. We order lunch—soup and salads—and take our meals to a table along the windows. Emily buys Sam a frosted cookie and I say that she's a better mom. "You know I'm going to eat half of it," she says.

I smile. "I'd do the same thing."

Emily glances at the screen of her insulin pump and I want to ask what it says, want her to explain how it works, its features and buttons, but I keep quiet. There doesn't seem to be enough time. The tables around us fill with older women lunching just like us.

Emily and I were girls together.

Many cultures believe that girlhood is something that must end in order to get to the next stage. I imagine that many mothers mourn this transition, this giving up and giving away. How many of them, like me, discover echoes of their own childhoods as their daughters grow up? I wonder if perhaps girlhood is something we still carry with us, like the Russian nesting dolls I keep on my bedroom dresser, and that without it, we cannot become women.

After her soup is gone, Emily starts scrolling on her phone. I tuck my apple in a napkin. I'll eat it in the car. Already I'm antsy to get back home, to be there when the girls step through the back door.

* * *

Once your daughters were so small that their entire bodies fit the length from your elbow to your wrist.

Once you drove with your friends. Windows down, heading toward no particular destination, music whipping your hair.

Once you were a little girl. Your mother made dinner each night and reminded you to brush your hair and teeth. Before bed, your parents stood over you. They pulled the blankets up to your chin, reminded you to be quiet—and then they turned off the light, hoped you'd be good.

# ACKNOWLEDGMENTS

This book is a testament to my memories. Some names and details have been changed to protect the privacy of real individuals, conversations have been recreated to the best of my ability, and in some cases, people have been left out. I am not capable of remembering everything that occurred or offering everyone's perspective, but the emotions and events described remain true to my story. Thank you for reading it and thank you to everyone who helped make the book in your hands a possibility. The process of putting these pages together has been one of the most exhilarating and trying endeavors and I could not have written it without the help of many kind and generous people.

Thank you Courtney Ochsner for believing in this project. It has been such a thrill to work with you and your team. The University of Nebraska Press is the best university press—full stop. I am honored to have this opportunity to collaborate and learn from all of you.

Katrina Noble's cover took my breath away. Natalie Jones, Abigail Kwambamba, Rebecca Jefferson, and Terry Boldan—your attention and efforts were invaluable.

Barbara Shoup read countless drafts and offered fabulous insights and pep talks galore. Thank you for understanding my story sometimes better than I did. Sarah Layden, Robert McNally, Susan Harness, Katya Cengel, Steph Auteri, and Sheryl Johnston offered edits and notes, and shared their expertise. Theo Nestor—your feedback gave me the fuel to keep going. Christine Sneed, Jody Keisner, Jill Christman, Dinty W. Moore, Michelle Herman, Abigail Thomas, Steve Edwards, Jeannie Vanasco, Anna Rollins, Jocelyn Cox, Eileen Drennen, Catherine Grossman, Mary Ardery, Jessie Glenn, Jo Ann Beard, Susan Neville, Brian Furuness, Michael Poore, Janine Harrison, Nicole Brooks, Andrea Boucher, Laura Kendall, Lauren Mallett, Tanya Perkins, Karis Pressler, and Emma Hudelson all left their mark.

To my students past and present—from Purdue University to the Lafayette Writers' Studio—it is an honor to read your words. Thank you for believing me when I said I was right there in the trenches with you.

I am grateful to the guidance of fellow creative writing colleagues at Purdue University: Josh Brewer, Casey Gray, Brian Leung, Don Platt, Catherine Shukle, and Sharon Solwitz.

I drafted these essays over several years and found the quiet to revise them during residencies at Taleamor Park, Trillium Arts, and at the Highlights Foundation. I am forever grateful for the gift of these creative spaces and the kind souls who devote themselves to making such places possible. Special gratitude to Heather Hartley, Phil Reynolds, Lisa Lee Peterson, and Clifford Peterson.

For love, friendship, and chats: Chris and Jenny—you are not just best siblings but my best friends; Sarah Anderson, Brenda Linley, Michelle Cooper, Katie Fields, Andrea Firth, Ada King, Erica Klaw, Mary Kenyon, Leah Lederman, Sue Sansone, VT, and Emily Umulis—I love you all.

My parents: You taught me to tell the truth, and I took that to heart. Thank you for support of every kind over the years and for skipping over some of the previous pages.

Last, my daughters Estelle and Josephine. When I think of the young women you are becoming, everything quickens. I love you so.

Pete: Thank you for more than I even know how to say. Somehow, with you, everything makes sense.

Thanks to the editors of the journals where these essays were first published:

"On the Verge of Being," *The Chattahoochee Review* 20, no. 2 (2000)
"The Facts of Life," *Northwest Review* 47, no. 2 (2009)
"Motherhood as Muse," *The Millions*, February 15, 2018 (section now appears in "The Perils of Girlhood")
"Deeper Than the Eye Can See," *Booth* 14 (Fall 2019)
"Cotton," *Pembroke Magazine* 51 (Fall 2019)
"The Sacred Disease," *Sundog Lit* 19 (Fall 2021)
"Vinegar," *storySouth* 52 (Fall 2021)
"Bad Blood," *Indiana Review* 43, no. 2 (Winter 2021) (retitled "More Like Dad")
"My Body, My Shame" originally appeared as "My Body, My Shame: Telling My Daughters About My Eating Disorder," *Your Teen Magazine*, January 3, 2022
"Lock Me!" *The Rumpus*, May 13, 2022
"To My Teen Daughters: You Don't Owe the 'Creepy Guy' Anything" *Grown and Flown*, October 18, 2023
"Under-prescribed," *Smokelong Quarterly*, June 19, 2023
"The Perils of Girlhood," *The Offing*, April 11, 2024
"The Telling," *Hippocampus Magazine*, May/June 2025
"Coach Matt," *under the gum tree*, forthcoming

# SELECTED BIBLIOGRAPHY

NOVEMBER 1, 1991

Chen, Edward. *Deadly Scholarship: The True Story of Lu Gang and Mass Murder in America's Heartland.* New York: Birch Lane Press, 1995.

THE SACRED DISEASE

Kaculini, Christian M., Take-Looney, Amelia J., Seifi, Ali. "The History of Epilepsy: From Ancient Mystery to Modern Misconception." *Cureus* 13, no. 3: March 17, 2021. https://www.ncbi.nlm.nih.gov/pmc/articles/pmc8051941/.

Kissiov, Diem, Dewall, Taylor, and Hermann, Bruce, PhD. "The Ohio Hospital for Epileptics—The First 'Epilepsy Colony' in America." *Epilepsia* 54, no. 9 (2013): 1524–34.

"Pathophysiology of Epilepsy." https://ksumsc.com/download_center /Archive/2nd/439/1-Neuropsychiatry%20block/Teamwork/Physiology /27%20pathophysiology%20of%20epilepsy%20.pdf.

ONCE, SOMETHING BAD HAPPENED TO US

Spellberg, Claire. "'Revenge of the Nerds' Filmmakers Address Controversial Rape Scene: 'I Regret That.'" *Decider*, July 26, 2019. https://decider.com /2019/07/26/revenge-of-the-nerds-rape-scene-regret/.

THE PERILS OF GIRLHOOD

Crenshaw, Paul. "What '80s Kids Also Remember: On Stranger Danger, Satanic Panic and Generations of Trickle-Down Fear." *Salon*, October 21, 2023. https://www.salon.com/2023/10/21/what-80s-kids-also-remember -on-stranger-danger-satanic-panic-and-generations-of-trickle-down-fear/.

LaFrance, Adrienne. "What Happens to a Woman's Brain When She Becomes a Mother." *The Atlantic*, January 8, 2015. https://www.theatlantic .com/health/archive/2015/01/what-happens-to-a-womans-brain-when -she-becomes-a-mother/384179/.

McLean, Carmen P., Anderson, Emily R., "Brave Men and Timid Women? A Review of the Gender Differences in Fear and Anxiety." *Clinical Psychology Review* 29 (2009) 496–505.

Valentine, Gill. "The Geography of Women's Fear." *Area* 21, no. 4 (1989): 385–90.

LOCK ME!

Cody, Dan. *Heritage Circle*. Pennsylvania: Western Pennsylvania Conservancy, spring 2015.

Gross, Daniel A. "The Forgotten History of Mace, Designed by a 29-Year-Old and Reinvented as a Police Weapon." *Smithsonian Magazine*, November 4, 2014. https://www.smithsonianmag.com/history/forgotten-history-mace -designed-29-year-old-and-reinvented-police-weapon-180953239/.

BARBIE STYLE HEAD

Adouké Doria. "The History of Makeup for Black Women: From Fashion Fair to Fenty Beauty." June 14, 2023. https://doriaadouke.com/from -fashion-fair-the-first-black-makeup-brand-to-fenty-beauty.

Bowerman, Mary, and Malcolm, Hadley. "Barbie's New Shapes: Tall, Petite, and Curvy." *USA Today*, WKYC, January 28, 2016. https://www.wkyc .com/article/entertainment/barbies-new-shapes-tall-petite-and-curvy /95–24259075.

DIABETIC VERNACULAR

Benfer, Amy. "The 'Sixteen Candles' Date Rape Scene?" *Salon*, August 11, 2009. https://www.salon.com/2009/08/11/16_candles/.

Grady, Constance. "The Rape Culture of the 1980s, Explained by Sixteen Candles." *Vox*, September 27, 2018. https://www.vox.com/culture/2018/9 /27/17906644/sixteen-candles-rape-culture-1980s-brett-kavanaugh.

Ranganath, Charan. *Why We Remember*. New York: Doubleday, 2024.

## IN THE AMERICAN LIVES SERIES

*To order or obtain more information on these or other University of Nebraska Press titles, visit nebraskapress.unl.edu.*

www.ingramcontent.com/pod-product-compliance
Lightning Source LLC
Chambersburg PA
CBHW020611270326
41927CB00005B/281